The Winding Stream

An Oral History of the Carter and Cash Family

A companion book to the documentary film,
*The Winding Stream — The Carters, the Cashes
and the Course of Country Music*

By

Beth Harrington

Praise for Beth Harrington's Work

Films

Welcome to the Club: The Women of Rockabilly [Grammy Award Nominee]

"A thoroughly entertaining ride . . . by turns funny, exciting, and well-researched"   — *Country Standard Time*

"A must-see, as four respective downfalls and comebacks are portrayed unflinchingly and without sentimentality."

— *Nashville Scene*

"Harrington travels the lost highway of American music history and comes back with a gem: the story of the fire-breathing, foot-stomping, fringe-shaking, rule-breaking, trailblazing women of 1950s rockabilly."   — *The Improper Bostonian*

The Blinking Madonna & Other Miracles

"[A] sophisticated mosaic of television and news clips, real-life videotape and actors reinventing Boston's North End . . . worth catching for its mordant sense of how a child of the 1950s creeps toward an acceptance of her past."   — the *New York Times*

"A gently off-center paean to the miracles of camaraderie and community, sensual pleasure and sheer human resilience — and an homage to deeply felt elements of her religious tradition."

— the *Boston Globe*

"Funny, touching, and winningly personal."   — *Chicago Sun Times*

"A crowd-pleasing hit . . . Fellini meets *Sleepless in Seattle*."

— *Boston Phoenix*

"Beneath *Blinking Madonna*'s intentional comedy, there's a quiet wisdom that makes the movie remarkably rich."

— the *Boston Herald*

Ave Maria: The Story of the Fisherman's Feast

"This skillfully made documentary portrays the deeper texture of a Sicilian-American community . . . outstanding for its visual and emotional beauty, technical excellence, sensitive narration and interview style, clear model of historical-social change, and its integrated coverage of the actions and feelings of many members of the community."   — *American Anthropologist*

"The story of the changing meaning of the festival for a community in flux. This moving, award-winning documentary makes an important contribution to Italian-American folklife studies and to ethnic studies in general."   — *Western Folklore*

Movable Feast

The historic film footage in black and white provides an appropriate visual metaphor for the dimming of memory. Color returns to the screen only upon arrival in Sicily. Here the American "bearers of tradition" return to the source, make a long pilgrimage, and see the Sciacca festival for the first time. The film allows us to hear what this encounter means from both sides. For the Italian Americans, it is gaining self-knowledge: why we do what we do, how we see life . . . For the Italians, it is knowledge of the other long-lost family members who emigrated."   — *Western Folklore*

Music

Jonathan Sings!

"Without the disarmingly precise backup of Ellie Marshall and Beth Harrington, Jonathan Richman's singing might have seemed merely eccentric."   — Robert Christgau - *Consumer Guide*

The Winding Stream:
An Oral History of the Carter and Cash Family

PFP, INC
publisher@pfppublishing.com
144 Tenney Street
Georgetown, MA 01833

February 2014
Printed in the United States of America

ISBN-10: 0991427505
ISBN-13: 978-0-9914275-0-5
(also available in eBook format)
Cover Design: Brian Murphy

ACKNOWLEDGEMENTS

This book is the result of almost a decade of interviewing for the documentary film, *The Winding Stream — The Carters, the Cashes and the Course of Country Music*. In that time, I was honored to speak with the members of the Carter and Cash Family and their close friends who were witnesses to and often participants in the events that shaped the groundbreaking music of the original trio. These people gave generously of their time and insights. For that and more I am grateful.

Thank you, Rosanne Cash, John Carter Cash, Laura Cash, the late Janette Carter, the late Joe Carter, Rita Forrester, Dale Jett, Fern Salyer, Flo Wolfe, Carlene Carter, Lorrie Bennett and Bill Clifton. I am particularly grateful to the late Johnny Cash who made a special point of granting his interview mere hours after he'd been released from a hospital stay and less than a month before he passed away. Though he probably was not feeling his best, he gave animated and impassioned testimony. It was a generous act done in service to his fond memories of his late wife June and mother-in-law Maybelle. It was a privilege to sit with him as he shared his deep feeling for these women.

I'd also like to thank the scholars who gave context to this project and the musicians who shared their appreciation and love of this music. Thanks, then, to Ted Olson of Eastern Tennessee State University, Kip Lornell of George Washington University, Peggy Bulger, the former director of the American Folklife Center at the Library of Congress and author Bill Crawford. A special thanks to the late Charles Wolfe of Middle Tennessee State University, whose extensive knowledge of the Carter story informs the film and this book, and to the late Mike Seeger, who clearly imparted his respect for the Carters in the reminiscences he shared. Thanks, too, to Randy Scruggs and Jeff Hanna for illuminating the story of the momentous culture-bridging album, *Will the Circle Be Unbroken*.

Thanks to my funders who made the film and this book possible with their generosity: Executive Producers David and Christine Vernier, the National Endowment for the Arts, the Virginia Foundation for the Humanities, the Fairy Godmother Family Fund, the Roy W. Dean Grant, and several hundred Kickstarter donors.

Finally, I'd like to thank my "best boy" Andy Lockhart for his love and support. You are the love of my life and the like of my day.

— Beth Harrington

INTRODUCTION

There is a stream that courses through American roots music. Its source is in the Appalachian foothills in a place called Maces Springs, Virginia. It was there that A.P. Carter, his wife Sara and his sister-in-law Maybelle began their careers as three of the pioneering stars of country music. From their earliest days as Victor Talking Machine Company recording artists to their international success via the phenomenon of Border Radio, the Original Carter Family made their mark on the history of American vernacular music.

These three didn't just play the music emerging from their hill country upbringing. They helped invent it. A.P. was both song collector and composer, crafting and arranging snippets of ancient, musty melodies, breathing new life into them and creating commercial American popular music. Maybelle took the then-underplayed guitar and made it into the cornerstone of country instrumentation that we know today. And Sara became the first well-known woman's voice in country music, stamping it with the eerie Gothic quality we find in so much of the country canon.

The stream these three created has turned into a rushing river and has moved through several generations of musicians, both inside their family and without. Arguably, there would be no Folk Revival of the '60s without the Carters, no country-rock bands of the '70s, and no alt-country hipsters of our present era. The Carters crossed styles, crossed genres, crossed generations.

And yet, the Carters suffered periods of obscurity, with A.P. and Sara divorcing and —— despite trying to keep the act alive — all three going their separate ways. A.P. died never fully realizing the impact he had on American music. Sara moved to California vowing to live a quiet life with her new husband, A.P.'s cousin Coy. Maybelle, fiercely devoted to music, struggled to envision what the next step would be.

The Carter story might have ended there. But it didn't. No one would have guessed that a young man who, at first blush, seemed more renegade than reverent adherent, would be the one to lift up the Carter legacy. That man was Johnny Cash, and his love for the Carter music dated back to nights as a boy in Dyess, Arkansas, listening to the Carter Family perform on the air (at that point featuring the next generation of Carters, including little June Carter), their melodies blasting across the Mexican border into his bedside radio. It was a wonderful twist of fate when Cash, as a Sun Records artist first met Mother Maybelle and her girls, the Carter Sisters and vowed to June that, "I'm gonna marry you someday."

The Carter Family legacy was upheld by Johnny, June and her sisters, Helen and Anita, and their cousins, Janette and Joe Carter. Then that torch was passed to the next generation of family members who would go on to perform and promote the music that their ancestors gave the world.

This book is the result of a decade of interviews with members of the Carter and Cash family and others who know and understand the legacy. It is in their own words, edited only for clarity and brevity. It is a companion to the feature documentary, *The Winding Stream — The Carters, the Cashes and the Course of Country Music*. The goal of this book and the film is to illuminate the foundation-forming history of this multi-generational musical family and honor them where they stand, at the headwaters of American roots music.

The Carter Family

Chapter One — The Originals

The saga of the Original Carter Family starts in a place called Poor Valley, Virginia. Life in this lovely but hardscrabble locale was a challenge. Nature almost always trumped human effort, whether it was farming tired land or keeping a home safe from wild animals or merely braving the elements.

It was into this environment that Alvin Pleasant Carter was born in 1891. 'A.P.' was a unique boy and an even more unusual man, full of tics and quirks and contradictions. He was capable of great focus but also someone who could become tremendously distracted. His family meant the world to him but his passion for music often undermined his familial duties. He aspired to be world famous but he died virtually forgotten in the remote enclave from which he rose.

Because of his complexity and the circumstances of his upbringing, many stories about A.P. Carter have an apocryphal quality. His beginnings were humble, his education rudimentary, but his aspirations were ultimately fulfilled. After his death, he would come to be recognized as a giant in American music.

BILL CLIFTON — Musician and Carter Family Friend:
How to describe A.P. Carter? I'm not sure I can. First of all, he had what everybody in the family called palsy. I don't think it was palsy. But he always shook. He had a sort of

nervousness about him. And that dictated a lot of how he was. He was always a little restless. He didn't sit comfortably for very long.

RITA FORRESTER — A.P. and Sara Carter's Granddaughter:
When my granddad's mother was actually carrying him, when she was pregnant, she was out picking apples and there was a storm coming. And lightning actually struck the ground and played around her feet. And she always said that that marked my grandfather. And he shook — from the time he was born, he had a tremor in his hands until the day that he died. And he only stopped shaking just a few hours before he died.

JOE CARTER — A.P. and Sara Carter's Son:
My father had a nervous condition. His hands shook. They tried to tell me that it was because lightning struck when his mother was carrying him, and he was marked by lightning. But I never did buy that. He had it all his life, the nervousness. Even in singing, it was in his voice — the quiver — just like his hands, they quiver the same way. He always liked to hold a songbook or something in his hands. That would quiet them down, I guess.

JANETTE CARTER — A.P. and Sara Carter's Daughter:
I've heard talk about Grandma Carter, when daddy was a baby and Grandpa was gone somewhere. They lived in a cabin and they didn't even have a window in the cabin. Where the window was supposed to be there was just a hole cut out. And they said there was a panther loose. And it was crying and she could hear it all around the house. And they say

Grandma Carter got a gun and laid it across her lap while holding the baby, and if that thing come through that window she was gonna blow it off the map.

FERN SALYER — A.P. Carter's Niece:
Around here it was a poor community. Not many people had much money. We were poor but we didn't know it. We had plenty to eat and our folks kept us warm but that was about it. Everybody worked hard. Even the children worked hard.

JANETTE CARTER: My father was a very kind man, very gentle man. But he had a bad temper when he got mad. Seems like he wasn't cut out to do an ordinary day's work. He had a lot of professions. There were a lot of things he worked at, like being a fruit-tree salesman. He had a gristmill at one time. He had a grocery store. He had a sawmill. Different jobs. He would go from one to the other. He sung in the church choir, he sung in schools.

FERN SALYER: He wasn't a great farmer. I know one of my neighbors said to me once, "A.P.'s not a very good farmer," and it irritated me that he'd say something about my uncle. And I said, "No, and you and I can't write songs either." And I was just a little kid and I told him that.

JOE CARTER: My Daddy didn't know nothing about farming. He'd make me get in there and plow when it was too wet. I said, "Daddy, that ground will be hard as a rock if we plow when it was wet like that." He'd say, "It don't matter, we got to get them weeds out of there." [*laughing*] He never did make much at the farming.

3

FERN SALYER: I could see him as a loner. If he was trying to come up with a new song, he was always in deep thought and a lot of times you'd pass him when he's walking up and down the road with his hands behind his back and it was almost like you'd say something to him and he didn't hardly answer you.

If something funny happened around him, A.P. didn't laugh. He snickered. He'd have a little silly grin on his face if something was amusing to him but he didn't really go "ha-ha." He didn't laugh like that. Something would happen and be real funny and maybe ten minutes later he'd just start snickering. And I have been told by his children sometimes this would go on a week or two. He would start laughing about something that happened without having talked about it. A.P.— you couldn't really read him. He was unique. He was different. He was A.P. Carter. That's about all you could say about him and we all loved him dearly.

Sara Dougherty, born in 1898, lived on the other side of Clinch Mountain in a place called Rich Valley. Her mother died when Sara was only three and her father, unable to care for his five children alone, sent Sara and her sister to live with an aunt and uncle. Some believe the trauma of losing her mother at such a young age forged Sara's character, making her an aloof and enigmatic presence.

From an early age, music was a balm for her and she displayed great musical talent. She began playing autoharp at ten, raising the money to buy the instrument by selling greeting cards. Music was pervasive in her aunt and uncle's home and throughout her extended family. She often played with her cousins, the Addingtons. But it would be talented little Maybelle Addington who, though significantly younger than Sara, would become her lifelong musical partner.

JOE CARTER — A.P. and Sara Carter's Son:
My mother was just blessed with musical ability. She played rhythm on a guitar most of the time or on autoharp. And she had her rhythm, her beats, right, you know. Her timing was precision. If Maybelle would get tangled up in the lead, she'd just listen and get with mother and she'd be right back on it. They call it band rhythm. She was gifted for that, you know. She'd keep the time. She had a good voice, my mother did. Had a wide range, she'd get on up high, and down low.

CHARLES WOLFE — Music Historian:
Sara did not have a mother telling her the proper way for a housewife to behave. I think Sara had a native intelligence about her that allowed her to see that there was more to it than this. And instinctively she was eager to find something out there beyond the typical life that her other friends had had. And I think that came about not by any kind of instruction or domestic wisdom, but that was just simply Sara being a brilliant creative artist and probably the smartest of the whole bunch.

I would love to have given her an IQ test. I think she would have blown the top off. Because she simply seemed to understand things — stuff that was hard for somebody else — like working up arrangements of songs and things of that sort. And in that respect it wasn't a case of nurture over nature, because Sara was just an exceedingly brilliant person who comes along every now and then in the most unlikely of environments.

JANETTE CARTER — A.P. and Sara Carter's Daughter:
My mother was a quiet, gentle person. Beautiful. She had the name of being very, very beautiful. And she had a voice like nobody else I've ever heard.

Maybelle Addington was born in 1909, also in Rich Valley. Maybelle's family was fun-loving; music played a central role in their lives. A story is told that Maybelle as a small child had managed to take an autoharp down from a table and begin playing by ear. Her abilities blossomed rapidly and she soon developed a reputation for fine musicianship. Besides the autoharp, she learned to play banjo. But it would be the guitar that would define her as a musical pioneer.

FERN SALYER — Maybelle Carter's Niece:
All the Addingtons were very kind and none kinder or sweeter than Aunt Maybelle. She was one of the greatest aunts anybody could have. And she was just one of the best mothers, of course, and one of the best musicians in the world but that never even entered my mind growing up.

But Aunt Maybelle she had such fun with children. She'd play with them and she'd tell tales and we were thrilled to death, cause she would laugh and giggle just like one of the children. She was just somebody you loved being around. She never made you feel unwelcome. She was always kind and I laughed going there.

RITA FORRESTER — A.P. and Sara Carter's Granddaughter: On my granddad's side of the mountain, people were extremely religious. Not a lot of frivolity, you know. My grandmother, his mother, Molly, did not even like him playing the fiddle, because they used it at dances. She wanted him playing a different kind of music: religious music or music that told a story, that had substance. But on the other side of the mountain they had a lot of fun.

That's where my grandmother Sara was from, and Aunt Maybelle was from. Aunt Maybelle's dad, he did some bootlegging. And they had parties; they had big parties, and danced, and all got together. Of course they did that over here on this side of the mountain, too, but it was usually at a church, maybe an ice cream supper. But over there they just got together to have fun. Really it was a different atmosphere. And I think when my granddad met my grandmother Sara she was probably just fascinating to my granddad. She was so beautiful and even until the day she died, my grandmother was one of the prettiest ladies you've ever seen.

And I'm sure that was part of the fascination, but just the difference in the way they were brought up. 'Course my Aunt Maybelle and my grandmother were first cousins and grew up pretty much together and were together a lot of their life, and were making music from the time they were little girls together.

And remained close all those years, you know, until they died. They just had a deep affection for each other. Later, Aunt Maybelle would go on to marry my granddad's brother, Ezra. So, there was a kind of double closeness there that other families maybe didn't have.

JOHNNY CASH — Musician and Carter Family In-Law:
When A.P. was a young man, he went over from Clinch Mountain to Copper Creek country, selling fruit trees. He had an old wagon, or a cart — I believe it was a cart. And he went over selling fruit trees to all the farmers along the way. He'd sell them fruit trees and then he'd sit on the porch and listen to their songs. He'd listen to their songs and then he'd write them all down. Write them all down and then he'd come back home and start singing and he taught them to Aunt Sara. And then Maybelle came along — and Maybelle and the three of them were singing the songs that he had collected over there. Some of them were old church songs that everybody knew. Some of them were songs that were obscure English and Scottish folk melodies, like "Wildwood Flower," like "You Are My Flower," like "Winding Stream" — some great songs that have their roots in Elizabethan music. A.P. found those songs in the mountains of Virginia and brought them to the studio with Sara and Maybelle.

CHARLES WOLFE — Music Historian:
When you look at the Carters as individuals, two of them are still sort of mysteries, I think, even to the family. Maybelle is one that everybody seems to understand, Maybelle was the kid. She was seventeen-years-old, and she was open and friendly, and able to get along with people. She was probably

8

— dare I use the word — the most "normal" of the three. A.P. was moody, he was puzzling to his family; he'd go off at times for reasons they didn't understand. He'd go out for long walks along the railroad tracks. He was quiet. If you look at the old photos, there's a burning intensity in A.P.'s eyes that is really almost spooky. It's the same kind of intensity that you see in the eyes of great blues singers like Robert Johnson; it's really there. And he was quiet. Nobody knew exactly what he was thinking at any given time. He tended to do things without telling anybody.

So, he's a bit of a puzzle. Sara on the other hand is, in my mind, the key person in the entire trio. Without Sara there wouldn't have been a Carter family. Not only was she a mother, and doing all the things that a young mother did in those days, a housekeeper, but she seemed to have this almost casual instinct to make good songs, and to create good songs. And yet it would be a mistake to think of her as a friendly, good time, southern farm wife. She was anything but that. She also had her own moodiness.

RITA FORRESTER: My grandmother, Sara, was so different from my grandfather A.P. Like when they say opposites attract? In their case, they were very different. She was quiet, affectionate but reserved with her affection, just very, very different from my granddad. It was hard for her sometimes to express her feelings. It was never hard for my grandfather, pretty much what you saw was what he was feeling. My grandmother was very reserved, very different. Not like most people's grandmothers. She was very liberated, used to doing things her way. She wore slacks when most women did not wear slacks.

<u>FLO WOLFE</u> — A.P. and Sara's Granddaughter:
Sara would go bear hunting; she killed a bear. She smoked cigarettes. She did do a lot of things that women in her day did not do. She went out and earned money. She went on the road and performed. Just very different from most, the stereotype that you have of a grandmother, just completely different.

<u>CHARLES WOLFE</u>: Back in the 1920's in Scott County, Maces Springs, basically the women would have been farm wives. They would have been expected to stay at home, tend to the kids. They had a huge amount of work to do because they were doing subsistence farming. There was very little money. I think I saw a census that showed Scott County was one of the poorest counties in Virginia in the 1920's in per capita income. The problem, of course, is that the countryside was so rugged that it was really hard to do any serious farming. So they would do food preservation; they would cook up apples, they would prepare things. They would engage in social activities built around the church. They would stay home almost all of the time. And they would devote their time pretty much to raising their kids. And this is what most of the friends and neighbors of Sara and Maybelle and A.P. were doing up there. It wasn't all that different from any rural family trying to get by in that day and time.

There was very little traveling. Many of the women probably never got out of the county that they were born in, and as a result didn't really have much experience with anything beyond that little world.

<u>FERN SALYER</u>: They were way ahead of their time. They were just special people, I think, that God created for us because we had nothing here and it was something special for the people here. But they never got away from the people here. They always loved it here and they always loved the people here. And they'd ask about everybody they knew. They never got above their raising. They just finally reached their potential, I think, of what they were supposed to be, what they were created for.

Mount Vernon Church

Chapter Two — Ambition

A.P. would frequently join Sara and Maybelle for the kind of impromptu music sessions that characterized the world of rural America before radio and record intervened. But his vision for them transcended pickin' parties at home. As A.P. cast about for a way to make a living with music, it became clear to him that together these three could go places.

CHARLES WOLFE — Music Historian:
The only kind of real music training that A.P. had, came from the gospel singing that he learned at the Mount Vernon Church and other churches. You need to understand that in the early days of the 20th century, a new type of gospel music was sweeping across the country. It was songs written in shape notes. This was a seven-shape note system that came out of the Shenandoah Valley in Virginia in the latter part of the 19th century. And the publisher of these songs would commission new ones to be written that were kind of lively and up-tempo, and more interesting than anything else, kind of personal. The old hymns were not at all personal; they were very general and very congregationally oriented. The new songs, had an awful lot of "I" and "me" in there.

So these new songs appealed to the younger generation. And in order to get these songs out, and into the churches, the songbook publishers like James D. Vaughan, who was located down in Lawrenceburg, Tennessee, would send out singing school teachers, and they would go to churches like A.P.'s. And they would conduct a two-week course in how to sing these shape notes, and they would also give you instruction in harmony and time, and all kinds of stuff you needed to work out the songs. And A.P. loved this, and his Uncle Flanders liked it, and as a result A.P. himself became perfectly capable of reading these song books. And he probably got his notions of harmony, and certainly his notions of arranging by looking at these books.

And he used more than a few of the songs in these songbooks later on to be recorded. For example one of his big hits in the 1930's was a song called "No Depression in Heaven," which was really a fine piece. And it was from a 1936 Vaughan Songbook. And the Vaughan Company had designed these to be sung by rather stiff formal quartets — four men and a piano or four men singing solo. And this was fine for a lot of mountain people. But what A.P. wanted to do was to loosen them up a little bit, to get a good two-beat rhythm on the guitar, to maybe simplify the lyrics. So what he would do is use the gospel training as a basis for what he was doing.

JOHN CARTER CASH — Maybelle Carter's Grandson:
When A.P., Sara and Maybelle began to work together on a regular basis, and they decided they were going to perform music, I believe that A.P. felt most comfortable in the gospel format because they were a vocal group. He didn't have to

hold back. He could sing the gospel there.

I think that it was of the utmost importance to my grandmother Maybelle, and to Sara and A.P. that they sang about their faith. It was this music that, I believe, meant the most to them.

It if hadn't been for the gospel songs, there would have been no Carter Family. If it hadn't been for the fact that they sang in church every Sunday, from when they could very first remember and learned parts and learned shape note singing, there would have been no Carter Family.

CHARLES WOLFE: Now the other side of the coin is that, of course, A.P. had known ballads all his life. And he knew how to sing ballads and knew the importance of the ballads. But in terms of actually creating a sound, it was these little old floppy-back songbooks. Those books are the secret weapon for the Southern harmony.

A.P. was the one who was able to take what was a fairly specialized type of music and make it appeal to a much broader audience. Let me give you an example of that. One example is his song "Will the Circle Be Unbroken." That came from a 1912 songbook. In there it was called "Can The Circle Be Unbroken."

The refrain was the same, but the verses were very different. The verses were very old-fashioned and stilted. And some people did them; we actually have recordings of people in the '20s doing them. But A.P. took a look at those verses and said there's no way. This is not going to work. And he created the famous verses, "I was standing by the window on a cold and cloudy day."

A.P. was the great arranger. He was the Billy Strayhorn

of country music. He knew just what to do, and what to do with it. A.P. had the band, in Sara and Maybelle, that he could hear what these things sounded like and whether they were any good.

MIKE SEEGER — Musician and Carter Family Friend:
His collecting of songs was done with great purpose. I don't think we really know who made those songs into Carter Family songs. But I think it was all three of them because they worked out their arrangements together since all three did different things with their music at the very beginning. As they became an act, they created a Carter Family style; three or four years into their recording career they'd sound pretty much the same all the time. Before that time you could sense a lot of experimentation both instrumentally and vocally but eventually they settled down into a style.

ROSANNE CASH — Musician and Carter Family In-Law:
Because it was just the three of them — A.P., Sara and Maybelle — by necessity Maybelle invented the Carter scratch, where she could play lead guitar and rhythm guitar at the same time. Maybelle was kind of playing these lead notes and the rhythm was in the background. Nobody else did that. She invented that, out of necessity.

LAURA CASH — Carter Family In-Law:
I've never heard a guitar player with a stronger hand. A stronger right hand. Maybelle's thumb looked like it was made of steel. There's a video of her on the *Flatt and Scruggs* TV Show, playing "Wildwood Flower." And the camera pans in on a close-up of her hand, her right hand. And that

thumb looks like it could just break those strings right off. It was so strong and unbelievable. And the whole time Maybelle's just smiling and making it look totally easy and effortless. Just so impressive. And I studied that video a lot when I was trying to learn her style. But Maybelle invented that style because she was originally a banjo player. She played a claw hammer thumb and finger picking banjo style. So when she picked up the guitar, that hand moved over to a different instrument, and that's where the Carter scratch came from.

The Carter scratch is a thumb playing the bass notes. And the finger — sometimes two fingers — playing the rhythm. It was really made to sound like two guitars at one time. There's a lead guitar going at the same time she's backing herself up. Which is unbelievable, really. Yeah, Maybelle Carter invented the Carter scratch. [*chuckles*] She's just a little petite housewife playing with that thumb just like a steel rod. Just unbelievable. And if you'll notice in that video, Earl Scruggs is behind her, just beaming with pride that she is on his show. He loved her. You watch Earl Scruggs play, he's playing Momma Maybelle-style guitar. He worshipped the ground she walked on.

JOHNNY CASH — Carter Family In-Law:
The Carter scratch did a lot for me, to begin with. When I was in the Air Force in Germany in the early '50s and trying to learn to play the guitar, the licks I learned on the guitar were Carter family licks. And that carried over onto my recordings at Sun Records in 1955. I used those same licks and kind of improvised and did my own thing with the electric guitar and all that. But it was the Carter Family.

<u>PEGGY BULGER</u> — Folklorist:
Maybelle was really the musician of the group. She's phe-nomenal. To this day there's the Carter scratch that every-body has to learn when you're learning early country music and it's her signature. She was also the first one I believe to really play the autoharp standing up and actually pick out notes on it.

She was such a great musician and Sara was the one with the strong voice.

Now what's interesting is A.P. was always so scattered. He'd come in sometimes and sometimes he'd forget his notes. Sara was really the anchor with her voice and then Maybelle would do the harmonies. A.P. just kind of stood around and piped up every once in awhile. So when you hear the Carter Family what you remember most is really Sara and Maybelle because you realize the guitar work is really great and the voices that you remember are the two women more than A.P., thought A.P. had a great bass voice that he contributes every once in a while [*chuckles*].

<u>MIKE SEEGER</u>: I have my own idea of A.P. Some people con-sider him whimsical, that he couldn't entirely figure out just what was on his mind and I think that's a good way of look-ing at it. But I think there were a lot of things that he did with great purpose.

For instance, people say, "Well, A.P. would just come in and sing once in a while." But if you listen to when he comes in and what he does when he does come in, you realize that there was an organization to that and he didn't hit any notes that were awkward. Whatever he did worked whenev-er he did it. In fact, I don't think of anything that I dislike about his bass singing — or his lead singing, which is some of the most touching country singing that I've ever heard.

CHARLES WOLFE: A.P. very seldom played anything, occasionally he played guitar. So when you really think about the limitations that a creative artist has, with two acoustic guitars, or maybe an autoharp and a guitar, Maybelle was a genius. She got different sounds out of every song. And she figured out ways to do her picking in ways that allowed her to keep a rhythm and a melody at the same time. She somehow figured out how to breakdown the melody into a skeleton of the melody. So she would play that way. She figured out ways to use extra beats in a measure; she was the first person in country music to do that.

Today the people in the Grand Ole Opry call that "a turnaround." And it's the idea that when you sing a verse you don't just simply go into the next verse. You play a little something, you do a couple of bars. And Maybelle was the first to do that. She was the first person to say, "Look, we don't need to be singing constantly every second on this record. Let's do a little something extra to set the mood." What filmmakers call an establishing shot. Maybelle liked to do those things. She would have liked to do an establishing shot, just to help make the thing work.

There's truth to the fact that Maybelle revolutionized guitar playing. It's hard to prove. But if you go back and you listen to phonograph records that had been made before Maybelle came on the scene, and even after Maybelle came on the scene, number one, there weren't very many people playing good instruments. They were playing cheap, beat up guitars that would never sound good under any condition.

But, they also were very stiff and they didn't tend to flow very well. They simply were not necessarily appealing. They tended to play in 2/4 time, just very strict, boring stuff. And what Maybelle did was she added a flow that showed that the guitar was not just a percussion instrument, but that it was actually a melodic instrument. And her picking style, the Carter lick, was something that gave a foundation to people like Chet Atkins and Merle Travis and the others.

Chapter Three – The Big Bang of Country Music

In the summer of 1927, Ralph Peer, a record producer for the Victor Talking Machine Company in New York planned a trip South to find new talent for the label. Peer targeted a town on the Tennessee/Virginia state line — Bristol. It was here that he discovered the Original Carter Family in a momentous recording session. That same week, Peer also signed the future yodeling sensation Jimmie Rodgers. Ralph Peer's finding these two seminal recording acts at the same time would compel historians to label the Bristol Sessions "the big bang of country music."

<u>CHARLES WOLFE</u> — Music Historian:
When the Carters set out in a car borrowed from Maybelle's husband Ezra, it was a hot summer day. Maybelle was eight months pregnant and A.P. and Sara had to bring their daughter Gladys along to care for her infant brother Joe.

There are two versions of the Bristol story. There's the legendary version and then there's the real version. The legendary version is simple: New Yorker comes into Bristol looking for talent. Carter Family crawls in through a window back of the studio, sings. New Yorker says, "My God, I've never seen anything like this, we'll make you stars." Records start coming out. End of story.

State Street - Bristol, Tennessee/Virginia

That isn't exactly how it happened. Like everything else, it is more complicated. First of all, the Bristol story is tied up with the idea that the record companies had gotten interested very recently in recording what they called "old time music." They didn't use the word "country" back in those days: it was "old time music." Actually, Victor called theirs "Native American melodies." But the idea was, it was kind of folk music from the mountains. And so, Ralph Peer was hired to go after this and find it. They had found a number of musicians, like Fiddlin' John Carson, and they had tried bringing them up into New York to record. And this didn't work out. It was expensive and most of the musicians didn't care to go to New York — surprise, surprise.

And then, in 1926, an event happened that really revolutionized all of this. Western Electric invented a carbon microphone, which was a much more sensitive way to make records. Up until that point, records were made with a big acoustic horn that was about the size of a room. And you would bellow into the horn and it would go down and cut wax. With this new electric microphone, you could record it almost like a regular microphone today. Well, that also meant that you could get all the equipment needed to make records into the back of a touring car. And when Ralph Peer realized this, he thought: "Oh, if the musicians didn't want to come to me in New York, I will go to them in the south."

So he took off in the summer of 1927 on a tour. And he went to Atlanta, he was going to stop in Bristol, he was going to stop in Charlotte, and, and I think finally in Savannah. But his idea was to go into these towns, set up a temporary studio, and try to lure people in for recordings.

And he arrived in Bristol in late July. And he was at the time not completely shooting in the dark. He had already corresponded with Pop Stoneman, with the Johnson Brothers, and other musicians who lived nearby, and said, "Look, I'm coming into town, we want to make some records, get ready." I think he had also met and corresponded with A.P. Carter. Because Cecil McLister, who ran the music store in Bristol, recalls that Peer had come down earlier in the Spring, and he had taken him out and introduced him to A.P. And Peer kind of liked the idea of recording A.P, and he had made a tentative agreement to do that. So even though Sara and Maybelle might not have known it, A.P. had in the back of his mind that he had deals set up. So Peer comes into town, and the first week he spends recording people he's already set up — the Stoneman family, the Johnson Brothers, and some others. Then he realizes, "Hey, I've got another week, and I really need now to go basically create cattle calls, and see who I can bring out." And he thinks about advertising.

In the meantime, this guy's been hanging around, a reporter from the local Bristol paper. And Peer thinks, like any good promoter, "Why pay for publicity when you can get it free?" So he invites this guy up to the session. So this guy does a couple of stories about the sessions, and everybody in the tri-state area reads that. Now, it could be that A.P. and Sara and Maybelle read it for the first time there. But I think they already knew they were going to be recorded. So what happened was they took off for Bristol. They were supposed to have gotten there in the afternoon. Even though it's not a very long drive to Bristol today, back in those days they had to go on what the maps called an "all-weather road."

And those all-weather roads, those were neat. What that meant was that they may have a little gravel in them, but they were mostly dirt roads. And so they had all kinds of problems: blowouts; they had to ford streams; it was hot. Maybelle was pregnant. And it was just a very bad time. And they had planned to get into Bristol and stay with relatives there in town and go over and do the session.

Well, they didn't even get to Bristol until that evening. But when they showed up, Peer said, "Come on over anyway and let's try to get some work done." And so their first sessions were actually held in a temporary studio down on Main Street. It was on the second floor of a hat company.

So Ralph Peer had made this warehouse into a temporary studio by hanging old quilts around the walls for baffles. They had a problem with the actual turntable that cut the record, because back in those days even though the town had electricity, the electricity was prone to fluctuation in power. And they couldn't very well make a master recording with the speed flowing and speeding up. So they built a tower and they rigged up a pulley on the third floor. They cut a hole in the floor, and the pulley would go up through the hole, up over it, and that pulley would therefore power the turntable. They had it timed so that they would put a couple of weights on it and when the weights started going down, it would pull the turntable for about three minutes, and the speed would be constant and equal — a very ingenious idea. Peer had with him a couple of engineers who were absolutely brilliant. And these guys were right on the cutting edge of electric technology. They were good; they rigged up a pretty neat thing.

So here we have the one microphone. We have a platform that the performers would stand on. Ralph Peer was in a little glassed-in room, and he would press a button, the light would go on red, and then when you press another button it would go to green and they would start singing. And they had been asked to make sure all of their tunes were less than three minutes. So, the Carters came in and after a few experiments, they placed everybody at the exact, proper space before the microphone because in those days, they didn't have different microphones for each singer. And they very quickly found out that Sara's voice was really powerful, so she backed up a little bit. When she played the autoharp, they needed to get a little bit closer. The guitar that Maybelle played was OK the way it was. And A.P. never did really sing very loud. He would kind of, as he said, do a little "bassing in" every now and then. Peer never quite understood that whole thing. But anyway, A.P. would stand in the back of them, kind of move around, and every now and then lean in and "bass in" a line or two.

So, they recorded four songs that night, including "The Storms are on the Ocean," and the "Poor Orphan Child" and Peer was very pleased. Four songs in about ninety minutes, no fixes or anything like that. They did do a second take on them — they were "safeties."

And what they would do is they would cut them into big wax platters — not cylinders. And they would cut the song into the wax, and when they got a good take they would take that wax platter out and pack it very carefully in cotton batting and get it ready to ship back to the company manufacturing place in New Jersey.

Peer was impressed. So he said, "We would like for you to come back and do some more songs tomorrow morning. Could you do that?" And they said, "Yes, we can."

So they went home and rested up. And the next morning about 9 o'clock, he goes in to meet the Carters. And lo and behold, A.P. has gone missing, and only Sara and Maybelle are there. And Sara says, "We can do the songs ourselves. OK?" And he says, "Well, OK." But he instructed his secretary who was typing up the notes from the session to put a note saying, "Mr. Carter not present." So Sara began singing her song "Single Girl." And that just absolutely blew Peer's mind. She sang it at the very top of her range, loud and striking — real mountain singing. And Peer had never heard anything like it. He said later on, "Once I heard her voice I knew that was it, I knew we had something very special." So they created a song that put them over the top just by themselves. And at the end of those two sessions, they were given a check, and sent on their way.

It turns out that A.P. was not there because he was out trying to buy a tire so he could have a decent tire to drive home on, and found one, and they took off back home. And they say that afternoon A.P. was back in his garden working away.

JOE CARTER — A.P. and Sara Carter's Son:
I was just a baby. I was nursing, you know, with my mother. I had to go with them if I was going to eat. [*laughs*] My dad didn't have no car, but his brother had an old '26 model Essex, and they worked out a trade, him and my uncle. My dad was gonna plant his corn out, if my uncle Eck would let him use his car, to take them to Bristol. And they took my oldest sister Gladys along to just take care of me. Get me outside. Beaver Creek goes down through there, you know. And she'd stand there and pull weeds up and throw them in the creek. And as long as I could see them weeds floating, I wasn't crying. I was interested in that you know.

And coming back, we had to ford the river down here. We did going over too. Coming back, that old Essex drownded out. You know, it got in the water and in the fan and she just coughed a time or two and quit. We just let it sit there awhile and it dried out to where it would run, and even the women had to get out and push. [*laughs*] And Daddy was steering it to get it out. And they was out there barefoot and pushing to get it forward and we got back home.

MIKE SEEGER — Musician and Carter Family Friend:
Can you imagine? From a small town in southwest Virginia, an eighteen-year-old woman, Maybelle, who can play the

guitar and sing with a baby due in a month starting her recording career? To me, that's an amazing thing to be able to do back then when there's dirt roads, there wasn't much electricity, you had a new marriage and a baby on the way. Whew, it took somebody like Maybelle Carter to be able to do that and to still have something to say to the RCA Victor people and to us.

<u>RITA FORRESTER</u> — A.P. and Sara Carter's Granddaughter: You know one of the stories about the Bristol Sessions was that the Carters came to the first session in bibbed overalls and barefoot. It's ludicrous. My granddad didn't own a pair of bibbed overalls and he never went barefoot. He would plow a field in a suit.

They went dressed in their Sunday best and it was important to him to present a wholesome family image and be always at your very best. So he didn't go to the Bristol session in coveralls. There was no way that he did.

Mr. Peer said that and the reason he said it was he was trying to sell the hillbilly image. He wanted them to be hillbilly musicians. That's what the music was called then, hillbilly music. And he even made some pictures of them in their work clothes. The ladies had on aprons out around the well and they had buckets, like they'd been washing and that sort of thing.

But my granddad didn't want those pictures published. He didn't want that image at all. That was what Mr. Peer wanted — the hillbilly image.

BILL CLIFTON — Musician and Carter Family Friend:
It was just before the Depression, but there wasn't a lot of money to be made here in Poor Valley. A.P. did a little farming and he did some construction work. And, you know, he picked up a dollar or two here and there, but he wasn't exactly flat out working.

And he figured that the music could produce some money also. And so he wanted to go to that recording session in Bristol. And neither Sara nor Maybelle really wanted to go, but they did. Of course, Maybelle was eight months pregnant, so her husband Eck wasn't too crazy about her going either. But they went.

And A.P. said that they looked around that building. And he said everybody was dressed to the hilt. They were all dressed up with fancy clothes on. And he said, "We just had our regular clothes on. And so when they called us to go, we didn't want to go through the main part of the building. We entered the studio, up on the second floor, by going up the fire escape, and went in that way. So people wouldn't see how we were dressed." Why he was ashamed of their clothes, I don't know. But I think he felt that the people with all the fancy clothes would think, "Oh, these people, they think they're going to get on records. Look at them. You know, they're just ordinary people."

But I know they were all dressed well. Because they'd stayed with A.P.'s sister Virgie and her husband Roy Hobbs the night before. They had a house in Bristol. And so, A.P., Sara and Maybelle had gone and stayed with them the night before. So they were all cleaned up and dressed up. A.P. never dressed in anything but a formal shirt. Usually a white shirt and good trousers and proper shoes, and everything.

And yet Peer wrote them up as being kind of country bumpkins coming in bib overalls. I guess he thought that would sell more records. But it was a little unfair to the picture of the man I knew and who the Carters were. They weren't those people. They were very particular about how they dressed. They cared about it. They were completely dignified people.

PEGGY BULGER — Folklorist:
I think that the recording companies were recognizing the fact that they had niche markets. They were not in it for anything altruistic or "we want to really have a cultural exchange here in the United States." No, they wanted to make money.

So there was a limited market for what they'd already done — symphonic music and opera and the great tenors and whatever. But there was this whole area that had been untapped as far as musical legacy is concerned and I think they were taking a chance. Peer took a chance and said, "Okay, let's go down and see what's down here," recorded it and waited to see if anybody would buy this stuff. And it was definitely the right thing to do. So not only did they start recording Anglo-American music from the mountains but then they had the Race records with black music from the Delta. All of a sudden Peer discovered that there was this huge market. The tip of the iceberg was what they had been recording. And they realized that there was much more music out there in the United States that had never been recorded and there was a market for it.

I wonder what would have happened, how long it would have taken for Southern music to make it. It would have been disseminated eventually but without somebody like Ralph Peer having the vision to say, "Gee, maybe we should see if this stuff would sell." I wonder how long it would have taken before people really got to hear this kind of music. It takes somebody, a visionary, I think, to go down and say, "Let's take a chance on this. This is really different music."

Sara, A.P., and Maybelle Carter

Chapter Four — Aftermath

After the Bristol Sessions, the Carters returned to Maces Springs, putting the experience behind them, satisfied with the money they'd made for making the recordings. Neither Sara not Maybelle had any expectation that the sessions would lead to anything further. But A.P. held out hope. Still, months passed without a word from Peer who, after Bristol, had been busy in other Southern cities making similar field trips for a planned series of records.

<u>CHARLES WOLFE</u> — Music Historian:
When the records started coming out, they were released as the "New Southern Series." And the Carters record was one of the first released. Big ads came out in the Bristol newspapers. HERE ARE THE NEW SOUTHERN SERIES THAT ARE RECORDED IN BRISTOL! And Mr. McLister, who ran the music store, wheeled a Victrola out on the streets of Bristol, and started playing the Carter Family, and Pop Stoneman, and all these others. And of course, he began selling records hand over fist.

A few weeks later, a check arrived in care of McLister. And Peer said, "Please take this out to A.P." Well at this point, A.P. apparently didn't even know the records were out. And he didn't understand that he had signed an agreement with Peer that not only would Peer pay him for making the records, but he would basically sign over the copyrights to Peer Southern. These records that they had done were really popular, and were starting to get recorded and performed on the radio. And so what this check was, was a check for the mechanicals. And McLister drove out to A.P.'s place and presented him with a pretty good-sized check. And it was only then that A.P. began to realize the way money could be made — that you made some money by going out and making records, but that the real money came from the songs themselves. And within about three or four years, Peer had a folio out of Carter Family songs.

By then, A.P. had become pretty good friends with Peer. They seemed to like each other. And the next time that Peer came down to visit, he wanted to visit with A.P. and stay a little while with him and talk about songs. And A.P. looked at his garage and decided it was too small for Peer's visit. So he built a garage just for Ralph Peer's car. The trouble is he didn't know what kind of car Peer had now. And when Peer got there and pulled his car in it was too small. About a third of the car stuck out the back end of the garage, which crushed A.P. He was horribly humiliated about that.

But he did have a good talk with Peer. And at that point Peer said, "Look, I think you are going to be making a lot of records. And I think it is to your advantage to take royalties rather than me pay you. The royalties will be a little bit more slow in coming, but in the long run you'll do better." So what happens is that A.P. Carter gets an education in the music business from the master, Ralph Peer.

Ralph Peer wasn't by any means acting out of the generosity of his heart. He was a hard-headed business man, and he wanted to make money and he was trying to figure out ways to do it. Peer recorded dozens and dozens of artists, and many of them were good for one record and that is really all they would do. But Peer felt that if he could cultivate a certain number of artists and develop a relationship with them, and treat them as business partners — equals — and show them how this whole system works, he'd not only have a source of songs, but everyone could make money.   People sometimes accused Peer of cheating the artists out of money. The way his company was set up he couldn't very well do that. He would have been in trouble himself. What happens is that a lot of lesser artists think they should have gotten more money because they can't imagine that their brilliant record didn't sell a million copies. But we know how many copies these records were selling — most of them were selling 5,000 to 6,000 copies. And when you realize that there weren't that many record players around in the south in 1927, that's not too surprising. What is surprising is when you compare that to the Carter Family sales. The Carter Family was selling 100,000 copies.

So Peer wants to treat A.P. Carter as if he's his star quarterback. This guy is the moneymen. He's the one who is going to keep these songs coming. And what was amazing is that Peer made constant demands for new songs, let's have another session. It was something that would never happen in Nashville today, where it takes two years to get an album out. Peer was asking A.P. to show up every three or four months with a bag full of new songs. And guess what, A.P. did it. He came up with good songs; the quality didn't fall. He didn't come up with junk songs. Some of the best songs

35

that he came up with were in those sessions. And when you listen to all of the A.P. Carter songs, and all of the Carter Family songs, you'll see that a lot of them weren't the big super hits. But even today when you listen to them they're awfully good songs. People could go to the Carter Family song bank, and mine it for songs that nobody's heard, there are still wonderful, interesting songs.

KIP LORNELL — Musicologist:
There are really two levels of song collecting. One — you have scholars who would go in and look for material.

But there's also another level going on in which people kept songbooks and ballad books of things that had come down through their community, come down through their family.

A lot of times people just collected what they were interested in and I think that's initially what A.P. Carter was doing. He was looking for the songs that he grew up singing around there. When it came to commercial recordings, one of the things Ralph Peer was very good at was putting his name on Southern music and sharing songwriting credits.

Now you can make of that what you will here in the 21st century in terms of intellectual property, but he caught on to that much more quickly than anybody else. So Southern Music and Peer Publishing over the years held some very important copyrights. They recorded the Carter Family and Jimmie Rodgers early on and Jimmie Rodgers and the Carter Family were prolific and some of their songs have gone on to be recorded by quite a few other people.

Peer, for whatever reason, figured out very early that it was advantageous to form a music publishing company, advantageous to have his name on there with other people and I think he instilled that in A.P. Carter pretty quickly. A.P. was no fool.

One of the old adages that's still true in song writing, it's not so much what you get from your live performances, it's the music publishing that makes you the money in the long run. And, boy, Peer and Carter figured that out early on.

RITA FORRESTER — A.P. and Sara Carter's Granddaughter: When those records started to sell and when Mr. Peer asked them to find more songs, to record more songs, then that started to put pressure on them to come up with material. And most of the songs they knew had, say, fifteen verses and Mr. Peer wanted songs that ran three minutes. That was what he had to have because of the technology of that time. The records only held a few minutes of music.

So in order to do that the Carters would have to rearrange the songs. They'd have to eliminate verses. A lot of times they might not have anything but just a verse. Maybe there wasn't a tune, maybe there was just a verse and they added the music. Certainly the arrangements were all done by my granddad and a lot of the things he wrote outright.

Take a song like "Cyclone at Rye Cove." He had to have heard about this tragedy and was actually over there and helped with the recovery and was moved from that because he saw the children that died in the cyclone. So, you know, he wrote that song about the cyclone.

But certainly the pressure started when the sales started and Mr. Peer wanted more. He wanted more music and he wanted them to come to a lot of recording sessions.

JOE CARTER — A.P. and Sara Carter's Son:
Music. That was my father's whole goal in life. He'd been standing around studying about a song, getting it in his mind. [*sings notes*] That's the way he would get his melody. He didn't want anyone carrying on when he was doing that. He wanted it quiet so he could concentrate. Once they formed the way they was going to do it, and stuck with it, it caught on quick, you know. People would come up to the porch, and sit on the porch and my dad and mother and Maybelle would sing. They'd get practice, and the people would get their ears full, so getting satisfied on both ends. That's kind of the way it was.

PEGGY BULGER — Folklorist:
I did my work on where the Carters got their songs from because as a folklorist there's a whole group of people who are searching for authenticity and, wanting to find the singers who are carrying on the old English and Scottish ballads, as opposed to people who are getting their songs from Tin Pan Alley.

Well, the Carters blew that apart. They gathered songs from any place they could find them. They were just like sponges. They would listen to things and then change them into their own style. They would reinterpret whatever they heard and so there was no such thing as authenticity; of course there never was. In a folk community, authenticity is, I think, a construct that scholars have come up with.

They had a remarkable career. They started in 1927 and they were done by 1941 — it was a very short career — but they recorded over 240 songs and most of those songs they copyrighted. Well, of course, we know that that was kind of the practice at the time. A.P. Carter would absolutely copyright every song that they reinterpreted.

So, as I was doing my research, it was very interesting because I found that they were kind of a microcosm of what people were listening to in the mountains. It was the first time that records had come in and people were actually listening to things that were fixed on a phonograph record. It was also when radio first came in and this was absolutely revolutionary. I mean it would probably be like when personal computers first came in. All of a sudden people didn't have to just hear live music. There was fixed music, there was music that was coming from far away — and those early radio stations could be way far away and the signal would carry. And so they were listening to things they had never heard of before. Local and regional music was breaking out into the national scene and the Carters were there at the right place at the right time.

The Carters were obviously also great musicians and they knew the music. But the other thing is that they were really adventuresome. They took their guitars, went in the car, and drove down to Bristol to start a recording career.

So I found over the course of doing my research that they had several songs that were old — what we call "Child ballads" [after Francis James Child, the American folklorist who collected them], the English and Scottish ballads that usually take twenty minutes to sing because there's five hundred verses and they're a story in song. They're all about lords and ladies and whatever.

Of course, in the Carter repertoire these ballads become very truncated because they had to be two and a half minutes long to fit on a record. So the story gets thrown out the window and they had maybe the beginning of the ballad and the end of the ballad and that's it.

They also took Tin Pan Alley songs. They took sheet music, old sentimental songs that people would have been singing in the parlor, gospel songs, shape note songs — you name it, they took it — and worked them into their own unique style. And those songs that they did that were put on both disk and then on the radio and became the versions that we now know.

So, for instance, most people know "Wildwood Flower" but most people don't know that that was "The Pale Aronatus" and that was a sheet music song from parlor music days. The song actually makes a lot more sense in "The Pale Aronatus." But because the Carters learned it through the oral tradition, they get the words all garbled up. So it really was, "I will twine and mingle my raven black hair with the roses so red and the lilies so fair." It makes sense that way. But the Carters said, "I will twine with my mingles and waving black hair" and that's the way that everybody sings it now because that's the version that everybody knows. So they had an enormous impact on music, enormous. People heard their versions of songs. Those songs then became part of our American repertoire. Most people know "Wildwood Flower" even if they don't know that it's a Carter Family song. Same with "Keep on the Sunny Side." I mean everybody knows that song.

It's interesting because from the very beginning people have been wringing their hands about the death of traditional music — "Oh, my God, Here comes the radio. It's the death of traditional music." "Here comes the Internet. It's the death of traditional music." Well, believe me traditional music is much stronger than that. It can outlast all of the new technologies and it has. It's just that culture never stays the same and the music's going to change but there's always going to be a whole spectrum of music from the most traditional to the most avant-garde and those things are going to influence each other. We've gotta get over that.

When the Carters first came to the scene, I'm sure it was absolutely astounding to them to be able to listen to music that came from Del Rio, Texas, music that came from New England. Ten years before that they would have never really had the opportunity unless they actually traveled down there or people came to their community and played in their community for them.

So, when they started hearing these things, I bet it was just like kids in a candy store because they were musicians and like sponges. They heard these sounds and thought, "Wow, this is really terrific." And they took these sounds and made them the musical icons that they are today.

BILL CLIFTON — Musician and Carter Family Friend:
A.P. said, "You know, I could just look at a house and say, There's a song up there. And I'd go up to these houses and sure enough, there would be songs. And people would sing them for us." But he said, "If there wasn't, sometimes people would say, "Well, no, but I tell ya what. We've got a piano stool full of the sheet music that you're welcome to." And so A.P. would take the sheet music. And sometimes they would just make a song from the sheet music.

CHARLES WOLFE: We have found many of the songs that A.P. Carter recorded in various old sheet music collections.

And what we find is that there will be a version, say of "Wildwood Flower" that came out in 1859, and it's obvious that this is, in one sense, a source for that song. But what we've got is a mystery in another sense. For while we have the sheet music at one end of the spectrum, we've got about fifty years there, in which that sheet music did something. And it's very likely when A.P. goes out and collects songs from people who, in fact, may have been singing them for fifty years, he didn't realize that somewhere back along the line, their great-great grandfather bought the sheet music.

A.P. would come home from one of his collecting trips, and he'd literally have his pockets stuffed with scraps of paper, of songs he had gathered from people down in Scott County or over in the other areas nearby. And these people really would say, you know, these are old songs, my granddad used to sing. So A.P. had no reason to think these are not traditional songs. And we don't know how those songs were changed by the people. We don't know how they looked when they came out of the copyright office. But after they had bounced around in the South for fifty years, some of them could have gotten changed quite a bit. Some of them may not have been, and it could be that A.P. changed them. So A.P. is basically a song doctor, but also a great song creator. And he would take some of these old songs and basically rewrite them. And make no mistake about that: A.P. was a genius at songwriting. He felt at the time that the songs he did had to have a kind of pedigree. He was a genius at spotting good songs, making them palatable, arranging them to be sung, and at times considerably rewriting them. And then there are substantial numbers of songs that he wrote from whole cloth.

So his work is really complicated as a producer of songs. It's not a simple case of him going out and getting old folk songs and bringing them back.

He was much more than that. He was a real genius at taking those songs and doing things with them and preserving them. I don't think he was thinking the way a folk song collector today would think, "Gee, this is wonderful old stuff and we need to preserve it for the sake of our heritage." He was basically looking for ginseng, — here's something that can be used and we can make a record out of it. And as a result, he produces stuff that's incredibly good and very memorable.

TED OLSON — Music Historian:
Some people have criticized A.P. in recent years, with the idea that perhaps he was co-opting other people's songs, that the songs were perhaps arguably owned by others. He was then, of course, borrowing and arranging, and then they were getting copyrighted in most cases under his name. But that of course considerably downplays his own genius as an arranger. And frankly he was growing out of a tradition where a lot of people were borrowing folk songs, arranging them, and publishing them to their own personal benefit.

That was being done in songbooks in the World War One years, and in fact before. There were a series of collections of mountain songs, or mountain ballads, on the American popular market, and some of these actually sold quite well. And in most cases, the arrangers would take the copyright credit for them — not that they'd claim to have written them, but nonetheless they would put "arranged by" and they would gain certain kinds of personal benefit from

43

them. In fact, A.P. probably had no clue as to the ramifications of this. He was kind of doing what was customary perhaps at the time, and he was loaning to these fragments of traditional tunes his unique genius as an arranger.

He certainly had a larger vision for this music, and as a person who could take things that were fragmentary and frame them and improve upon them, I think most people would say, until he had a well-shaped song that ultimately loaned itself perfectly to the burgeoning popular music recorded sound market that people like Ralph Peer were pioneering. Of course Ralph Peer was the one, not A.P., who was really encouraging songwriting royalties being paid to his musicians. Because if Ralph Peer could be the publisher, he could share in the benefit of this.

And so it was just common practice in the recorded sound industry, and it was also common practice among song collectors of that era. Most people acting as song collectors didn't understand what we understand today about the need to be clear about separating the collector from the collection.

We've been able to benefit by many years of ethnographic documentary study becoming its own field, and I think our consciousness is much different about this, and the ethical responsibilities of the documentarian. Those responsibilities are very different today than they were in that day and time. And of course, A.P. was operating in a popular entertainment industry, and was taking what he felt in some ways was culturally his birthright, because this music — these song fragments and these melodies and such — were being sung around his community as he was growing up. In many cases, he used material that must have seemed well within his cultural birthright.

And so, really the ethical definition has changed in the intervening years. We have to be careful not to be too quick to judge somebody like A.P., given the time and place where he was working, and I think we should ultimately be grateful that somebody with his unique genius at arranging took these fragments of texts and tunes and sculpted them into songs of everlasting merit.

PEGGY BULGER: You have to take things in context of the times and back when A.P. was going around and collecting songs, first of all, it was kind of unusual. But he had the foresight to go ahead and copyright their version of the songs, which actually is absolutely legal even today. You can copyright your own version of a song. It's a fixed recording and you can do that.

I don't think there was ever a thought in his mind that he was stealing anybody's songs. I think he felt like he was collecting them as kind of a raw material and then shaping them into his own version of a musical performance which then is copyrightable.

I believe that he did enough rearranging and adding to a song to make it absolutely his. When he was taking a song whole hog, I have heard of him paying people for their songs, with the recognition that, "Hey, this is a valuable thing. I'm going to give you a payment for it and then, I'm gonna use it." And, in many ways, that still goes on today. If you're going to make a recording you're going to copyright your version of the song, even though it's in the public domain or whatever. I don't think we can judge A.P. by the standards of today.

I think that today if he was an ethnomusicologist or a folklorist, if he was going out in the field he would have release forms and a form to share any kind of royalties, if they were going to make a recording. But, back then, there was no conception of that.

<u>CHARLES WOLFE</u>: The crucial thing about A.P. is that he was a very natural man, and by that I mean that he looked at his valley, and what he wanted to do was to figure out ways of taking elements of that beautiful environment up there and make a living with it. So he farmed for a while, he did sawmilling for a while, he did all kinds of planting. And a cultural element of that environment were the songs. And as far as he was concerned, he was harvesting a crop. He was taking songs. And he was such a genius that he knew not to take the bad ones, and believe me, there were plenty of bad ones he must have run into. And he knew exactly what would work, and he would gather them down and bring them home.

And then the second stage would begin. He would show them to Sara, and then later on to Maybelle. First of all it would be Sara. And Sara and Maybelle would sit down, and you can imagine them saying, well, here's this song he brought home, what can we do with it? How can we make it work? And they would make it work — they would shorten lines, they would reverse lines, they would simplify lines, they would add beats, they would work out a guitar accompaniment, and they would turn it into a masterpiece. So it was a wonderful little mini-production line, and it produced great song after great song after great song.

Chapter Five — Song Collecting

As A.P. Carter faced the demands for more material, he expanded his song collecting searches. These trips took him into the African-American community of Kingsport, Tennessee. There he met a group of blues musicians including a guitarist named Lesley Riddle. Lesley impressed A.P. with his playing and intriguing song choices. On the spot, A.P. invited Lesley to his home in Maces Springs. It would be the beginning of a long association based on a mutual love of music.

KIP LORNELL — Musicologist:

I think one of the things that attracted A.P. to Lesley Riddle was the fact that Riddle was local and that he knew material like "Cannonball Blues." It was kind of an adventure for them going out and finding songs together and I don't know if it was kind of an illicit adventure because they were black and white going out together. I think it was a little bit unusual because there's certainly a power dynamic there with race. But I think that was evened out somewhat by the fact that Lesley Riddle was a good musician, he knew other musicians around town and he was also, I think, comfortable dealing with a white person, in a way that you simply wouldn't find in the Mississippi Delta. That would have been a very different dynamic all the way around.

47

Musicians Brownie McGhee (left)
and Lesley Riddle (right)

A.P. Carter was not color blind. He lived in the segregated South, not as segregated as, say, Canton, Mississippi maybe, but segregated nonetheless. So what he did was a little bit odd but in the context of where he was living — Southwest Virginia/Eastern Tennessee — going around with somebody like Lesley Riddle to collect songs was not an unusual thing.

In fact, ethnomusicologists John and Alan Lomax did something similar with Huddie Ledbetter [aka Ledbelly] when he got out of prison in August of 1934. Ledbelly spent that next fall going around with the Lomaxes to southern prisons as kind of an ambassador to the other black musicians. So some of the better songs that were collected in prisons by the Lomaxes were done with Huddie Ledbetter paving the way. So this was not a unique thing. But A.P. and Lesley Riddle were doing this before the Lomaxes did it and it was with a slightly different intent. It was with a more commercial intent.

A.P. Carter was looking for good songs. Lesley Riddle provided him with good songs and I think they got along well, too. That was one sense that I got from talking to Lesley and also from Janette Carter and some of the other members of the Carter Family over the years. A.P. spoke fondly of Lesley Riddle. And I think the fact that they were similar in age had something to do with it, too.

CHARLES WOLFE — Music Historian:
Lesley Riddle used to visit with the Carters, was a guest in their house many times. And he showed Maybelle a lot about the blues, and even showed her how to play the slide guitar, which she does on several numbers. And so once she got these basic instructions down, and once she got a really

good instrument, like that big jumbo, she herself didn't lose any time in figuring out things that could be done.

RITA FORRESTER — A.P. and Sara Carter's Granddaughter:
The Carters were influenced by all different kinds of music. My granddad, A.P. Carter, would go anywhere to hunt down a song and he didn't care where he went. If he thought there was a song there, he'd go and be gone for weeks at a time. He never hesitated to go to the homes of black people to find good songs and most of the best gospel songs came from black community. He would often go into their homes and when he would go and stay and be there late in the evening, he'd spend the night with them. There were no hotels and he didn't have any place else to go so he'd go and visit with them, see if they knew any old songs and move on and visit some more folks and see if they knew any old songs.

And then of course one of the big influences on him was Lesley Riddle who's a black musician from Kingsport. Lesley taught Maybelle a lot on the guitar, taught them a lot of gospel music and they were heavily influenced by the black music that they ran into song-collecting.

And in later years they were influenced by the music of Mexico when they were on XERA radio. Maybelle did a lot on the guitar influenced by the Mexican musicians.

So A.P. picked up things everywhere they went.

There were so many things that they were influenced by and they never closed their mind to those things. They were always receptive to them and so they never missed an opportunity to hunt for a song or to find the right song.

MIKE SEEGER — Musician and Carter Family Friend:
I've only met two people that went along collecting with A.P. and the person I got to know the best was Lesley Riddle. We don't even know exactly when A.P. met Mr. Riddle. But what I think happened — I have to say, this is my opinion — is that after the first or second recording session, by the reception of their music and the sale of their records, A.P. was encouraged by Mr. Peer to go out and find more songs.

The Carters knew plenty of songs but I guess A.P. felt that he needed to go out and find more songs and one of his trips took him to the African-American community in Kingsport. Why he went to the African-American community I'm not exactly sure, but I'll bet the Carters had records of people who were black. They undoubtedly liked all kinds of music.

Eventually A.P. met Lesley Riddle who was part of the community, where blues musician Brownie McGhee and some other musicians lived, and they struck up a friendship. Lesley Riddle would visit and stay with A.P. and the family in Maces Springs, which was not an everyday occurrence, I would expect, because as far as I know, that community was pretty much European-American.

I remember Lesley told me that he showed Maybelle how to play the country blues style where you play the melody in the top strings and accompaniment in the bass. It's the reverse of what Maybelle's style was, where you play the melody in the bass and you strum in the treble. Lesley Riddle showed her that country blues style. Lesley said, "You don't have to show Maybelle very much." I'm sure she picked up real fast. And Lesley learned to play the mandolin while he was there. He showed them songs and they learned them

51

and he also learned some songs from them. Enough so that he's not clear on whether he learned a song from them or they learned that song from him — and he had a pretty good memory too.

That song "The Cannonball" they learned from him. A.P. bought that song from him or traded it for something Lesley needed at the time, according to Lesley.

And then A.P. asked Lesley to go on trips with him, to go out, collect songs, and Lesley said he was the "Polly parrot." He learned the tune and A.P. would get the words. And I don't know whether A.P. wrote these down or not. I would have thought he'd have to. I wonder if there's any of those ballads or written manuscripts around?

Lesley would be the driver and they had a pretty much up-to-date car by that time and they'd go far and wide. I think he went up to Charlottesville once which in those days must have been a four or five hour drive at least and on not very good roads some of the time. And they had various, shall we say, biracial experiences, because you have white A.P. Carter and black Lesley Riddle and then you have to find a place for Lesley to stay overnight and they'd find him families mostly to stay with because that's the way it was done then.

I can't imagine what it was like for a white guy and a black guy to go collecting in the country because they would go to both white and black homes, I assume. I don't know that for sure but I would think if they did it in Kingsport they would do it other places, too. There are all kinds of wonderful things to wonder about and we'll just continue wondering about some of those.

I feel some of the songs would be affected by Lesley's

way of singing, which was different from the Carter Family. Phrasing and the way you get from one place to another in a tune is style, really, or a large part of style. So even though Sara had her own style, she would be somewhat affected by the influence of having learned a song from Lesley.

Another time I remember Lesley talked about collecting with A.P. down in Georgia and they wanted to stop and get something to eat. So they stopped at this roadhouse and as usual A.P. would go in the front door and Lesley would go to the back door. And Lesley went in the back door and they told him they wouldn't serve him back there. So Lesley went back to the front and said, "Mr. Carter, they won't serve me here." Without a word Lesley said they both left. Got in the car, turned it around, and headed back home. To me that was a big thing for A.P. to do. It spoke very nicely to me about that relationship.

Mike Seeger was a member of a folk trio called The New Lost City Ramblers. In 1963, they sought out Maybelle Carter and asked her to play some gigs with them in the Southwest.

MIKE SEEGER: We first heard of Lesley Riddle when we took that drive with Maybelle from L.A down to Tucson. We began asking where she learned some of those songs. She said, "Oh, I learned that from Lesley Riddle."

I tried to find him down around Kingsport. Got lots of bad leads and then I was talking about this with Brownie McGhee at a gig we had. He said, "Oh, yeah, Lesley Riddle. He lives up in Rochester, New York." So I went up there and looked in the city directory and there he was: Lesley Riddle.

Lesley had a CD on Rounder Records and he was a wonderful singer. His guitar playing was a little rusty by that time because he didn't play much anymore; he was in his sixties. But he was a wonderful singer and he's a good guitar player.

Lesley Riddle was physically big — he was six foot, I think, and a broad-built man. He'd lost a leg and a couple of fingers in an industrial accident. He was very well spoken and thoughtful. He just did whatever he could do for employment. He worked in a barber shop and as a school crossing guard.

In the South there's a lot of crossover of gospel and secular music. There's always been, for hundreds of years, a musical communication between white and black. So, I'm not surprised this happened with Lesley and A.P. It just took a couple of exceptional people to do it though because there can be fear on both sides. There's fear on the white side that you're gonna be accused of being friends with the black person and then there's fear on the black side, too, of being hurt because you might be too friendly. So it takes a certain way of being, in my estimation.

KIP LORNELL: When I met Lesley Riddle I was probably about nineteen or twenty, this was 1972 or '73, shortly after I graduated from high school. But I knew enough to drive from Albany, New York to Rochester, New York to interview this guy because I thought he was important.

And he was pleased that anybody was interested enough in his music to come three or four hours to interview him and he was also pleased that somebody knew enough about that kind of dynamic to ask him, I think, pretty reasonable questions.

Now he played music a little bit but he was clearly out of practice. He hadn't lost his facility. He could certainly play but he wasn't somebody who could sit down and record a lot of selections without some practice.

He was a very genial and very pleasant guy.

The sense that I got from talking to Lesley about the song collecting was they would do one of two things. A.P. would drive and they'd usually go to a section of town where Lesley Riddle knew people and they would simply go around and listen to songs. Or they'd take off and just stop and talk to people. I think it was primarily going with people that Lesley Riddle already knew because he knew a section of town that A.P. didn't. He was privy to a world that A.P. was interested in because he knew that there was a whole world of black American music that could be a gold mine of material. But even as a white man in Bristol he wasn't quite able to go into the same places as Lesley Riddle.

They were doing some collecting of all kinds is my understanding. Even though the black population around the Bristol area near Maces Springs was significant, it was still small enough and it was still segregated. Most blacks you could find in a particular section of town, although in more rural areas you'd find blacks in smaller areas that were family farms or small communities of blacks. It was pretty easy to know where to go to find musicians.

Upon their return from these song collecting trips, A.P. and Lesley would meet with Sara and Maybelle to share what they'd gathered. Often the songs were fragmentary. Sometimes they'd return with lyrics or poems, sometimes with melodies that Lesley would remember.

Lesley would teach Maybelle the guitar parts — "Cannonball Blues" being probably the most dramatic example. The Carter Family has always acknowledged Lesley Riddle as the basis for that.

It makes me wonder how much Lesley might have influenced the Carter picking style in general because I have the sense that they would sit around for quite a while just playing.

So there was enough camaraderie that Lesley would have been welcome there just to hang around and play music for a while. Those kinds of informal sessions, in addition to very directly transmitting some of the songs that A.P. and Lesley learned and refined would have happened in a relaxed situation, hanging out there just playing music.

Lesley would stay with the Carters. He would hang out there for a while because he was a man with relatively few responsibilities at that time. He didn't have a lot of kids hanging around, he wasn't married. This was something he liked to do.

When I met Lesley Riddle it was decades after the fact. So you have to realize that he was caught somewhat in nostalgia — a nostalgia for the South, a nostalgia for an older friendship, but it seemed like a very genuine nostalgia.

The perception I had from speaking with Lesley about his relationship with A.P. is that it was less of a black-white dynamic. "I happen to be black, they happen to be white but we like the same kinds of music." This was social and musical interaction that occurred on a very friendly and familiar level. They lived in fairly similar circumstances, they lived near one another. They were sharing music and I don't think it was a business dynamic by any means.

Who could predict the Carter Family would become the dynasty in American country music? They were just local folks. They liked the same kinds of things and I think that's really what drew them together.

In the 1920's instead of working in an agrarian situation, Lesley worked in a cement plant and at some point there was an industrial accident that injured his leg which had to be amputated.

It wasn't a career ending injury but it maybe got him to thinking about things he wanted to do more. I think that's one of the reasons why he wanted to focus on music more. "Yeah, hey, I'm not going to be around here forever. I'm going to do some of the things I like" and when somebody like A.P. came along maybe that was just added incentive for him to become more involved with music.

I think the Carter Family are somewhat unusual in a number of regards in terms of the material that they used. One is the fact that they did rely upon song collecting and upon people like Lesley Riddle for part of the repertoire.

What also makes them unusual is they recorded so much from the late '20s up through the early 1940's. They had to come up with new material and that forced them to cast a wider net going back to songs they would have sung in church, songs that they would have gotten from hymnals, songs that they would have picked up from the Pentecostal Movement, songs that they would have picked up from neighbors — songs from all kinds of sources.

So in a large regard they really looked far and wide for blues influenced material, gospel material, popular songs of the day, topical songs, because don't forget how important somebody like Vernon Dalhart was with his topical material which sold tens of thousands of phonograph records. That had an impact on what they did, too.

I'm sure Ralph Peer also helped to shape the Carter Family's repertoire as well. He wanted them to record a wide variety of things and probably encouraged them to keep recording religious material. It's hard to underestimate how important the sacred section of the Carter Family material was. You basically have popular songs, religious songs, and a healthy dose of topical songs about tornados, about floods, the kinds of things that they would have seen around them. That's part of what they thought they should be doing at the time.

Song collecting was a critical part of the Carter Family's musical success. But it also proved to be a source of conflict. As A.P. traveled the South searching for material, Sara was left to deal with whatever arose on the home front. It would be the undoing of their marriage.

LAURA CASH — Carter Family In-Law:
A.P. was gone a lot. He was walking over the mountain, walking up and down the valley looking for songs. He was very serious about the Carter Family's career. He was also just a wanderer. He couldn't stay put for very long.

Meanwhile, Sara was raising the three kids and just having to do all the work. She was cutting wood to keep the house warm, to cook and to bring in water and who knows what else. Anything that needed to be done, Sara was the one that had to do it. And she got tired of that, after years and really just developed a lot of resentment there, I think. And that couldn't be undone.

She also didn't like the life in the spotlight as much. She also resented that. She felt like she was being made to do that. She would rather be home, be a family.

BILL CLIFTON — Musician and Carter Family Friend:
A.P. was somebody who was just so dedicated to the music. And he wanted to get out there and play and go anywhere he could take the music. And he just knew it was good for people, that this kind of music was a good thing and that people needed to have that in their lives.

I know that A.P. was so dedicated to the music that he would get up and leave the house. I've been told by members of the family that one February he got up and left Sara at the house on the mountain with no wood for the fire, no money to buy any groceries. He said, "I need to go find some songs," and just up and left. And there she was with three small children. No way to make a fire, middle of winter, and no money to buy any groceries. And he just didn't think about that. He was thinking about the music all the time.

Of course, many people said, "Well, yeah, what woman can do that?" I mean, naturally that would lead to a divorce eventually. But I don't think A.P. ever thought of that. And, of course, he was in love with Sara till the day he died. He always hoped that Sara would come back. It was a dream he had. And he talked about it a lot. He'd say, "I think Sara will come back, you know."

But A.P. had blinders on when it came to music. And he didn't see left or right. His music — that's what he wanted to do. And he could not balance those things that needed balancing in his life.

LAURA CASH: Eventually it was just too hard for Sara. So

A.P. had asked his cousin, Coy Bayes to help while he was gone, look after things, take her on errands, fix things. And Coy and Sara spent a lot of time together and they ended up falling for each other. And it changed everything.

Coy was A.P.'s cousin and no one knew how to feel about it. So Coy's family just packed up and moved to California. There was nothing that was going to save A.P. and Sara's marriage at that point. The damage had been done. The marriage was broken.

Sara went back home to the other side of the mountain.

RITA FORRESTER: My grandmother needed more security and that lifestyle was not conducive to security. They were traveling all the time. She wanted to be at home. She wanted a life with her children and that just wasn't gonna happen if they were making music so that was really hard for her.

I do not know all the details about their divorce. I guess growing up all that we knew was that it hurt my granddad to talk about it and therefore we didn't talk about it 'cause I loved my granddad. So everyone of us just knew that it was not something we were to discuss. They did have differences that they could not come to an agreement on.

And so when Sara left Maces Springs, she actually went back across the mountain and lived where she had lived before with her Aunt Nick and Uncle Mil for about six years before they finally divorced. And it was she who actually finally divorced my granddad. He did not divorce her.

They really did continue to care about each other. I guess it was in an odd way and in a way that people didn't understand but my granddad never stopped loving her till the day that he died and to a large degree she loved him, too. She just could not live with him. He was difficult. He could be difficult. He had a temper and he liked things to go his way. He was used to having things go his way.

The Carter Family in the Border Radio Years

Chapter Six — Border Radio

Though A.P. and Sara divorced in 1936, it did not mean the immediate end of The Carter Family musically. Ralph Peer pushed hard to keep them together as an act. But even without Peer's encouragement, none of them really needed to be told that music was a decent livelihood, and one not available to most people during the desperate Depression years.

The Carters were selling records, but records alone were not enough to provide a stable income in those years. Because Sara and Maybelle had small children, touring was difficult. So when they were offered a steady stint on a radio station in Texas, A.P., Sara and Maybelle jumped at the chance, even though the first season meant leaving their children behind in Virginia. And of course, Sara and AP's divorce did not make the transition an easy one.

RITA FORRESTER — A.P. and Sara Carter's Granddaughter: By the time the Carter Family went to Texas, A.P. and Sara had divorced. They really tried to work their problems out. They made a real effort to do that for their children's sake, I think.

And of course, Mr. Peer persuaded them to keep working together because they were selling a lot of records and he wanted them to continue working together. And they always had a good relationship when it came to their children. They always tried to agree when it came to their kids and when they were singing they were in accord. You know it was just that the rest of their life was hard.

The Carter Family sold enough records then but they didn't make hardly anything. It was half a cent for each record, which is really not a lot. Of course, they would get paid when they did the recording and then the royalties would come from the number of records that were sold.

But when you look at the number of records that were sold, it was phenomenal for the time considering that it was the Depression. I imagine they might have done better had they gone on the road but then they would have had to leave their family and that was something they never wanted to do.

That was one reason that my mother Janette and Maybelle's girls, Helen, June and Anita went to Texas after the first season. Sara and Maybelle could not bear to be apart from their children. They didn't want to be. And it was important that it'd be the whole family together. So they always stuck together whatever they did.

CHARLES WOLFE — Music Historian:
The funny thing about the Carter Family, and their career after Bristol, is that there wasn't much of a career. Jimmie Rodgers — the other person who recorded at Bristol – very quickly got booked on the RKO vaudeville circuit; he was doing movies; he was traveling around all over the country. While he was doing that, A.P. was nailing up posters onto trees and barns for locally produced concerts that he was

doing. The amazing thing is as popular as their records were — and they continued to sell way up into the Depression — they didn't seem to be able to exploit it the way a group today would. The traditional method is you have a big hit record, you go on tour, you support it, and you get out there and make your real money that way. And for reasons that aren't entirely clear to me, they didn't quite get a handle on that.

You have to remember that in the 1920s and '30s, being a country music singer wasn't really an accepted career. It was not accepted for several reasons. One was that there were a lot of people who looked upon it as something faintly immoral, especially with two ladies going out on stage. And there was the idea of people actually making money by singing southern folk songs. That just didn't quite fit. So, the idea of a professional country singer hadn't really taken hold yet. Jimmie Rodgers –— when he got on the vaudeville circuit — eclipsed the idea of a country singer. He was basically almost a vaudeville entertainer. But the Carters could never have done that. You couldn't take the country out of them. And as a result they did not reap the benefits they should have reaped in the 1930s. They were comfortable, and they were able to live well. But A.P. was still scrambling and doing things to try to keep the family together.

Peer was supposedly their manager. And I think part of the problem is that Peer was so busy with his other things that he wasn't really looking after their career the way he should have been. I think had they had a better manager they could have gone on the vaudeville circuit. They could have gone out and made some big time money.

Finally, Peer did get them on a radio show contract in

the 1930's. And they signed a contract with the Consolidated Drug Company, and did some transcriptions, which were basically big records that were used in radio shows. So a station could say, "The Carter Family is on this station every day at noon," and they could play one of these big transcriptions and the Carters could be doing something else. And the Carters wound up going to XERA on the Texas-Mexico border — once again a good contract, a good weekly salary. Finally, ten years after they make their first hit records, they're starting to really get enough money to make a living at what they're doing on Border Radio.

RITA FORRESTER: Mr. Peer convinced them to go down to Mexico and work for Consolidated Drug and basically help with Dr. Brinkley's advertisements, which had to be interesting for them. It had to be a complete shock to their system, not anything they were used to.

Of course, it was the beginning days of radio. They were pioneers in everything they did, radio, recording, the songs, everything. They were pioneers. They were breaking new ground. No one had done this before.

But part of the appeal in going to Mexico and to Texas was that they could work six months and be home for six months and yet they got paid the year 'round so that was a real incentive for them and that was a deciding factor in going to Texas.

Well, my granddad liked it at first. He loved being in a different place.

And I think my grandmother Sara actually enjoyed Texas and Mexico. I know that Maybelle was distressed over leaving the kids that first season. You know she did not want to leave the kids and I know Maybelle's youngest, Anita, said that they would listen to the radio and she would cry because she thought her mom was actually in the radio and she couldn't get out.

And I remember her saying that for a long time she did not like Jimmie Rodgers because she thought Jimmie Rodgers had something to do with her mother not being with her and she would actually do bad things to his phonograph records because she thought he was part of the problem.

So they sent for Anita right away and I think my mom Janette was the same way. She was distraught so she went too. Mom was just sixteen-years-old. Eventually they all ended up going.

The Carters stayed at a boardinghouse on the Texas side of the border. And there was an opera singer who lived one level above them and Anita would listen every day and imitate that opera singer. She was only six-years-old but that's how she developed her incredible range, by imitating that opera singer.

Life on Border Radio was a real big transition for them but they tried hard to keep a semblance of family life. They all had their meals together and, of course, the kids had to go to school in Texas. The kids out there made fun of their mountain accents and there were no Methodist churches where they were. So everything was different; it was probably a big adjustment for them.

BILL CRAWFORD — Author:
Border Radio refers to super high-powered radio stations that were built on the Mexican side of the U.S.-Mexican border by outlaw broadcasters back in the early 1930's when

radio broadcasting was in its infancy. Now you may ask, why would they go to Mexico to build their radio stations? Well, one of the reasons was that the U.S. government formed something called the Federal Radio Commission, which later became the FCC. And the FRC started doing things like regulating what you could say on the air, and what power you could run your station at, and what frequency you could run your station at.

So a few broadcasters went foul of the FRC and had their license removed, and had to go somewhere to get around the US government regulations about broadcasting. So one of the first people to have this license removed as a broadcaster was a gentlemen by the name of Dr. John R. Brinkley. Brinkley was one of the great mavericks and innovators in American broadcasting history. He had his medical degree from the Eclectic Medical University of Kansas City. He was a doctor of Eclectic Medicine. And he started to practice medicine in the tiny town of Milford, Kansas. Now, in the early 1920's, Dr. Brinkley perfected the operation that I like to call an early version of Viagra. And Dr. Brinkley called his operation "the goat gland proposition".

And what Dr. Brinkley did, was he took a small slice of a goat gonad, and inserted it into a man's personal area. Now, Dr. Brinkley did many, many of those operations on many famous people all around the world. One of the people he operated on was Harry Chandler, publisher of the *L.A. Times,* and a variety of other individuals. He made a lot of money.

Soon, he had a big clinic, one of the biggest clinics in the Midwest. And in order to entertain his patients he built what was then kind of an oddity in the early 1920's — a radio station. So he could sit in his office and give medical lectures over the air. And the station grew and his practice grew along with it.

But when the FRC was formed, one of the first people they threw off the air was Dr. Brinkley, for his questionable medical practices, and also for the fact that he would diagnose diseases over the air and recommend his own patent medicines that he had druggists sell. So Brinkley lost his station and he was kind of at sea as to what to do.

But he got a letter from Del Rio, Texas — this little community down on the border — saying, *"Dr. Brinkley, why don't you come down to Del Rio, set up your clinic, and build your station across the Rio Grande in Old Mexico, the little town of Villa Acuna?"* So, sure enough Dr. Brinkley moved down there in about 1931 and built a Border Radio station — XERA — on the Mexican side of the border. And he was outside all the regulations of the FRC at that time. He could broadcast on any power he wanted to; he could say anything he wanted to.

Dr. Brinkley hired some of the finest engineers in America to build this radio station. And they said, "What power do you want?" He said, "Build it as powerful as you can." So the ultimate, the highest power that a station licensed by the FRC could have was 50,000 watts. Well, Dr. Brinkley's station was 250,000 watts. And they built a directional antenna on it, so that the effective radiated power going north was a million watts from XERA — a million watts of power.

So this was the most powerful broadcasting station in the world at the time. It was the most powerful communication tool in the world at that time. It was the internet of that era because you could hear this station literally all over the world.

So Dr. Brinkley built this huge power station, and he started letting people advertise their products. And really, these border stations were really the pioneers of modern broadcasting. They were the first ones to use per inquiry advertising. They were the first ones to let preachers on the air ask for money, because you couldn't do that on regular American radio. They were the first ones to really popularize country music. They were the first ones to allow music that wasn't kind of "high toned" and high class to be on the air, and they were the most powerful radio stations on earth.

One of the biggest sellers of medicines on border radio was a guy named Harry O'Neil who worked for the Consolidated Royal Chemical Company. And he was one of the fellows who was selling Peruna — a cold tonic — among several other products.

So Harry O'Neil had Peruna and was trying to push it on the air. So he looked around America to try to find the people who will appeal to his clientele: people who are rural, who like country music, who like the old style gospel-y music. And he found them — The Carter Family.

So Harry invited the Carter Family to come down to appear on the Border Radio station, XERA, in the season of 1938, and he actually paid them $75 a week to perform. So they were the royalty on the Border Radio station. Once they got there and played on the *Good Neighbor Get Together* they really started pulling the mail — as many as 25,000 letters a week to this little station in Del Rio, Texas.

Brother Bill Guild was the host, a very religious guy who started being the announcer for the Carter Family mainly because he thought he could bring people to religion by speaking over the largest broadcasting entity on earth. And he could. And he'd introduce every show and say, "Well, welcome to the *Good Neighbor Get Together*, we're all glad to have you here, and here's that good old Carter Family to sing for you: A.P., Maybelle, Sara, Janette, June, Anita, and Helen and, of course, they'll have to sing that good old theme song for you, 'Keep on the Sunny Side.'"

But these big transcriptions the Carter Family recorded and sent them to stations, not only played on XERA, but XELO, which was in Tijuana, and they extended to XEG in Monterey, which was one of the most powerful Border Radio stations.

Now, like so much of Border Radio, we've heard stories about this power. Supposedly this station was so powerful that birds flying near the antenna would fall from the sky dead. We've heard stories that people living near this station didn't need electricity; their light bulbs went on by themselves. We've heard that people could hear the station on their bedsprings, on barbed wire fences, and even on the fillings in their teeth.

JOE CARTER — A.P. and Sara Carter's Son:
The place was so hot with electricity at those border stations. The transmitter was right there, the tower and all. You could just touch a barbed wire fence, and it would burn you — the heat — it wouldn't shock but it would burn you. It just heated up like an element on a stove or something.

A fellow had a radio made; I couldn't believe it when I first saw it. What he had was just an old tin can, like an old tomato can. And he punched two holes in it, and run a wire through it — a naked wire — and stretched that wire up to the roof and tied it off. And set that up on a piece of flat iron. And you could listen, and you could tell what was playing in the radio station. I could tell when my folks started their show and when they ended. I could tell what they announced. That's just how hot the station was.

BILL CRAWFORD: It was great having the Carter Family kids on the air because they really appealed to the listening audience. This is the very early broadcast years. There is no television, there is no internet. People would gather around and "watch" the radio. That is the biggest show in town if you are on an isolated farm. And families love to hear kids. So the Carter kids were some of the child stars of the era really.

JOHNNY CASH — Carter Family In-Law:
When I was a boy living in the cotton country in Arkansas, at night after working in the fields I would listen to the border radio stations, as well as WJJD in Chicago, WLS, and all the other stations that played what they called hillbilly music. But the first time I heard the Carter family was on border radio; I mean the first time I heard them live was on border radio, the transcriptions they played that they had recorded there. And I thought it was wonderful music. I had my ear right in that radio. When my dad would yell to go to bed, I would just turn the volume down but put my ear closer, 'cause I had to hear the Carter family. That's when I learned to love the Carter family, when I was a boy.

BILL CRAWFORD: So the Carter Family and now, their children, were performing on the *Good Neighbor Get Together*, playing live on XERA, and they were also making transcriptions of their performances to play on other Border Radio stations — to distribute them. And these were electrical transcriptions, but they looked like big, oversized records made out of aluminum, and they would play from the inside out.

The Carter Family's performances kind of reflected what was happening in the family at the time. It wasn't a happy family. There was a lot of sadness. There was a lot of heartache. A.P. and Sara were split up at this time, and you could really feel the tension in their performances on the show.

LAURA CASH — Carter Family In-Law:
Sara was very unhappy at the Border Radio station and out of the blue one night she sent out a song to Coy Bayes, "I'm Thinking Tonight of My Blue Eyes." She hadn't talked to him in six years and just wondered if he'd be listening. Border Radio, of course, transmitted all over America and sure enough he heard it. He was with his parents in California and came in and told his mom and dad, "I'm going to get her." So Coy loads up and drives to Texas and takes his bride and they were married within a week.

JOE CARTER: My daddy, he didn't approve of that, you know. He hated it. That other man was his first cousin.

FERN SALYER — A.P. Carter and Sara Carter's Niece:
I remember the day that Coy and Sara got married 'cause Joe was back home then and he came to our house and I heard Daddy ask Joe if they'd gotten married and Joe said, "Yes." And I think Daddy said, "Was A.P. upset?" And I think

73

Joe said, "Yes." I was young but I remember thinking that's why Joe came over here. He was very young. And divorce back then was . . . you just didn't hear of it and not in that family.

It was a very close family but it was inter-tangled sort of, too.

I would never say who's at fault, who's not at fault. I loved all of them. I just loved Aunt Sara to death, always did. She was always Aunt Sara. Till the day she died I just loved her. Nobody blamed anybody. Just difference, a lot of difference in them. I know A.P. was gone a lot. He wasn't home and she was there with the children.

RITA FORRESTER: I guess I never heard my grandma's side of things because obviously she was in California most of the time. She visited about once a year and, as I said, it was something we never discussed, even with my granddad or with her.

In looking for pictures of the cabin is actually where I came across what I think is one of the most beautiful photos of her I've ever seen. And it's her and her family probably just before her mother died. She was about three, I imagine, very small, and she's standing between her mother and father and she has her hand rested on her mom and one on her dad but she's not smiling. And to me it was just very sad and it made me stop and think about what growing up without her mother must have done to her and how hard it must have been when she actually did leave and leave her children.

Growing up without your mom would probably make you cling to your children even more but I think when she left she was thinking of what was best for her children at the time. And she knew that her children, with their father, had a wonderful support system; they had his mother, they had his sisters, they had basically what they needed. And I guess she knew that they had everything that they needed and that she could not give them that.

She had to spend a lot of sad years wishing that she was with her children. I know being a mother myself there's no force on earth that could take me from my children, nothing, and I know she must have had to feel that way.

But growing up without her mom had to have left a very big void in her life and probably left her never secure, never in her whole life. When you have all that taken away from you and then to not even be with her dad. Her dad kept her brothers but actually had her and her sister go to an aunt to be raised.

That would make you somewhat insecure, I suspect, and I imagine she might have been more secure had she stayed with her father, although he probably thought he couldn't raise those five children on his own. And at that day and time men didn't raise children on their own.

Men just didn't do the nurturing of the children and people didn't divorce in those days — at least not here. It was unheard of. They just didn't do it. They stayed together no matter what.

I think a lot of people judged her very harshly. Of course, she married my granddad's first cousin which completely broke his heart. Sara and Coy actually married in Texas while the Carters were performing on the radio. And then, she moved to California which is where Coy lived then.

I'm sure she was judged very harshly by a lot of people

and I imagine that's one reason that the distance gave her some comfort. She wasn't judged as harshly there.

CHARLES WOLFE: With Border Radio, the Carters were finally able to see some money from something besides the record royalties and song royalties. But still, you feel like it wasn't as much as they should have.

The Border Radio experience was in some way a kind of cusp in their career. Sara left at that point and moved to California with Coy Bayes. A.P. went back to Maces Springs. Maybelle was the only one of the bunch that really saw the future in professional country music. And once she got her kids to where they could sing pretty well, she immediately took off and started forging her own career — first on the Old Dominion Barn Dance, then later in WNOX in Knoxville, then the Grand Ole Opry. At which point, she'd really become a full-fledged professional entertainer.

The Carters tried to get back together in 1941. They had a chance to get a contract for a station in North Carolina. And A.P. persuaded Sara to come on back on the train, "Let's give it one more try, and see if we can get a really good contract and make a decent living."

So they were on WBT Charlotte for a number of months, when something happened at the time that looked like it was going to be their big break.

A photographer from *Life* magazine heard about them, and decided that they wanted to do a feature on the Carter Family. The family and the photographer went up into Maces Springs and shot pictures. The problem was they were scheduled to run that story in *Life* magazine in the December the 7th, 1941 issue.

BILL CLIFTON — Musician and Carter Family Friend:
The Japanese bombed Pearl Harbor and the story didn't run.

My theory is that the Carters were bombed out of their career, basically. I think if that *Life* Magazine had come out, as planned, there would have been an incredible amount of work for the Carters, all over this country, because *Life* went everywhere. It wasn't an Eastern or a Southern magazine, it was a universal American magazine.

And, if it hadn't been for the bombing of Pearl Harbor, and the fact that that issue was never published as planned who's to tell what the Carter Family career would have been?

CHARLES WOLFE: And we can only imagine what might have happened had that issue been published. All of a sudden big national advertisers find out about the Carter Family. With the war starting up, their kind of sentimental, honest, straightforward songs, songs of home. They would have been great. They would have been heard overseas. They would have won thousands of new fans all over the country. But it didn't happen.

And so after that, A.P. went back to Maces Springs and Sara went back to California.

RITA FORRESTER: Music put a lot of demands on them that other families did not face. I think my grandmother never wanted a life on the road. It wasn't as important to her. She did it, and her voice was certainly part of the magic of the group, but it was never as important to her. She was quite

77

content to go off on her own and not be on the road. Now, Aunt Maybelle loved it. And my granddad would have gladly done it all his life. But when the Original Carter Family broke up, it took part of my granddad's heart. He had put so much into it that it really was a very sad thing for him.

Chapter Seven
— Mother Maybelle and The Carter Sisters

When the Border Radio era ended and other possibilities for the Carter Family faded, Maybelle Carter was at a loss. Unlike her sister-in-law Sara, she loved touring and performing and had no intention of giving it up. Besides, Border Radio had been a training ground for her three daughters, Helen, June and Anita. The four of them were turning into an act of their own.

Fortunately, Maybelle's husband Eck — like his brother, A.P. — had a bit of the show biz impresario in him as well and began to devise a plan for his wife and the girls.

LAURA CASH — Maybelle Carter's Daughter-in-Law:
Eck was home and I think he saw the handwriting on the wall — that this work was about to end with the Carter Family. And he started thinking about how things were going to change if his wife wasn't working. [*chuckles*] So he started realizing, "Hey, we can do this. We've got Maybelle, three girls that are talented, and they could go on the road." So he started booking shows for them. In the beginning, Eck ran the whole deal. He booked their shows, and drove them, and managed them. He took on that role. He was a very intelligent man. He was a great dad and a great husband. And he really did support the family, and the music. He knew

what the level of musicianship, their level of fame and what the possibilities were. He knew the potential. And he was really supportive of keeping that going.

LORRIE BENNETT — Maybelle Carter's Granddaughter: Grandpa definitely encouraged or pushed them. He said, "Maybelle, you take those girls and you get out there and go for it!" So, that's what they did. He pretty much managed them and got them out there. He made the deals.

Mother Maybelle and the Carter Sisters

LAURA CASH: I do believe that it was Ezra's idea to put Anita on the bass and Helen on the accordion. There's a funny story that Helen just could not get the accordion. She just was frustrated with it and didn't like it. And it's huge and she was a skinny little girl. And she's trying to figure it out. And she played piano, so it made sense to him that she could take this mobile little piano on the road. And, they played a show with Pee Wee King, and Pee Wee said, "Helen, you know, you got that thing on upside down." After that, it was much easier for her.

Then Ezra put Anita on the upright bass. And she was not even ten-years-old. So, they had to have her stand on a stool to be able to play it. But this was all his idea again. Ezra was the entrepreneur of the bunch. He knew what was gonna work and what wasn't gonna work. And he knew that we had to have a well-rounded band with a rhythm section. Maybelle was gonna be playing the guitar. We needed a bass player. And we needed some lead instruments as well.

FERN SALYER — Carter Sisters' Cousin:
When Maybelle and the girls decided to go on their own, they had been rehearsing. And everyone would say, "June wasn't a singer." June would say, " I'm not a singer" and she wasn't a really great instrumentalist either. You know, Anita had this great voice. Helen could play anything and June was right. She wasn't that good. But she had the stage personality that everybody loved.

One day my Daddy [Eck and A.P.'s brother] comes in and says, "Well, they figured out what they're gonna do with June. June is gonna be a comedian." And he said, "You know she's really good. She's funny." I remember that. That was the beginning.

JOHN CARTER CASH — June Carter & Johnny Cash's Son:
My mother always had an amazing sense of humor. She was

a funny lady and a funny little girl. And she had a wit and a charm that was unlike anybody else in the world. And my mother had persistence in her nature. She had life and light. She wasn't afraid to say exactly what she thought. But even early on, I think that she figured, I've got to make my stance, and I've got to stand in the middle. I'm gonna sing the part right in the middle and do the best I can. And she wasn't afraid to sing. I think that was a big thing for my mom. Even though she didn't have the angelic voice of Anita or didn't have the guitar talents of Helen, she had courage like no one I'd ever seen. She was not afraid to get up and sing to the world. And she could make people laugh. And in all these things, she was granted a million pardons.

FERN SALYER: As a child, Anita was totally spoiled rotten but as sweet as she could be. She was so cute and she was the youngest. And they had her singing when she was so little that she'd have to lay in the guitar case and sleep when they went to do shows at the radio stations. They'd just wake her up when it was her time to sing. She never really had a normal life like her sisters. She had a hard time jumping from the music world when she was young. She wanted her own life I guess.

But there is no greater voice. She could do it all. She could hit the high notes that nobody could touch and she did with such a beautiful sound. She really had more of a pop voice. She never fulfilled her potential to the limit, I think. She never pushed her career.

Helen always loved the music business. Helen was willing to go anytime, anywhere to entertain. But June was the one that really pushed things.

CARLENE CARTER — June Carter's Daughter:
Helen was the glue. She made everything work. If anything was missing, Helen could play it or sing it. She was like Grandma in that sense. She was probably the best songwriter of all of them. In fact, she really influenced me. When I first was starting to write, she taught me a lot about songwriting and would write songs with me. It didn't matter whether anybody had ever heard them. Didn't even matter. Helen loved it better than anything. But she was one of those people that could pick up anything, kind of like Grandma, and play it. Now, the funny thing about Grandma and Helen was that they bickered all the time, almost like sisters. But they loved each other deeply.

On stage, Helen and Anita hardly ever got to get a word in edgewise with June around. June did all the talking. So Helen and Anita kind of got a little bit of a short stick; people didn't get a sense of who they were.

I've never seen anybody rehearse so much, in my life. [chuckles] They loved to rehearse, them Carter girls. And, to this day, I have to remind myself when I have to go into work mode and I need to rehearse, I think of how they rehearsed. That's why they were good. They loved rehearsing.

Maybelle loved playing and perfecting her technique. The thing about her guitar playing that always killed me is that she sticks these tiny little fingers in there that make it Maybelle. Anybody can play the melody and play a rhythm. She sticks these little rhythmic things in there and makes it special. And it's hard to figure out how to do. You have to sit there and study your entire life to ever do it exactly like she did.

She was most comfortable, I think, in her life, when she

was playing her guitar or her autoharp. And, I can't say that she was an "entertainer," you know, like June was an entertainer. I consider myself an entertainer. People that go out there and go, "Hello, how ya doing?" Grandma really wasn't like that. But the thing about her is, as soon as that first beat was supposed to come and she was supposed to play it, she would beat herself up if she didn't get it just right. She was really a perfectionist about it, and she instilled that in Helen and Anita and Mom.

With Mom, there was no way to kind of lasso her talent. It just kind of went everywhere and did what it did, which was fantastic. Grandma was very driven by perfection and her craft. And, that's what I really liked about her. But at the same time, she had like this naughty little sense of humor. And, if she told a joke that had the s-h-i-t word in it, she just thought she was getting up to no good. And she would laugh and laugh and laugh.

But Maybelle did have a dignity about her, too. I think it was a little unnerving how quiet she could be. I think people would get thinking that any minute she's just gonna go off on them. She didn't do that kind of stuff. But she kept everybody in line.

LORRIE BENNETT: They loved life on the road. Even when they were sick, at their worst, the spotlight would hit them and they'd be fine. They loved it. That was their life from the time they were children and even Grandma from the time she was a child — face it, she was a child when she started, you know. And that's the only life they knew.

The road was just something they enjoyed. It took them two or three days to get packed to go, but they had everything with them. They had every kind of safety pin, every kind of colored thread, every needle size — you know just in case. They had everything imaginable. And everything was in zip locked bags once Ziplocs came out.

They were prepared for anything when we was traveling in cars, or we didn't have room for the luggage. When we were gone on the road, Rosey, Carlene and myself — this was back when we were little kids — the luggage would be in the floorboard where the hump was on each side. And then they'd fix this little palette. We were down there on the floorboard on that palette. But the luggage was there — had to have that luggage — and then it was packed in the back.

And then later on we started carrying a trailer behind us. And then they moved on up, you know a little later on, to bigger, nicer vehicles to get more people, more luggage in . . .

CARLENE CARTER: There were these elaborate networks of trusses to keep all the Carter women together. Trust me. There is underwear involved. It's all in the underwear. It's like we all have these dresses and these outfits and stuff we wear. But if you don't have the right bra on, particularly, or you don't have the right undergarments, things could go horribly wrong.

And it's always been about that. I mean, Anita had an eighteen inch waist. And she had a girdle on. Don't ask me why.

So it's kind of that old thinking about momma and her pantaloons. Don't show too much. Lift your dress up, but don't show them nothing.

<u>LAURA CASH:</u> When Maybelle and the girls went on the road with Ezra driving them and managing them, it really was a pretty brutal schedule. And Ezra had a lot of to take care of back home. So they started interviewing musicians.

Chester Atkins was a guitar player and they met in Knoxville, on WNOX. He had his own show. I think he had actually been fired a time or two from the show. And the Carters just really liked him. They remembered him from WNOX and they called him to do some shows. So they took him on the road and he worked out real well and got along with everyone. He started doing some of the driving and Ezra was able to stay home some. So naturally, Ezra was thrilled with this discovery. And Chet was a great musician, and he brought a lot of new material to the band, too. He had them branching out on some jazz standards and taught them a lot as far as the musicianship goes. To the girls, he was like the brother they never had. He also played the fiddle on the road with them.

After Ezra got the girls started on the road, he was able to book a lot of shows with this fresh new band that was the Carter Family still but, at the same time, was kind of the next generation.

Chet always gave the Carters credit for his beginnings. He said, "If it weren't for the Carters, I wouldn't be here." He gave them all the credit.

<u>CARLENE CARTER:</u> Chet Atkins always said — to other people but also to me — that he learned a lot about playing guitar by listening to Grandma play.

LAURA CASH: There's a great story about when the Carters — Maybelle and the girls — were invited to play on the Grand Ole Opry. And I think there was some behind the scenes politicking going on with the union musicians — they knew about Chet Atkins. And I think they probably just didn't want him to get too close to Nashville, because he was so good. And so they invited Maybelle and the girls to come play at the Opry. And the manager of the bunch, Ezra Carter, told them, "Well, we'll be bringing Chester with us. He's part of the band." And they said, "Well, actually, he's not invited. We just want the girls and Maybelle."

LORRIE BENNETT: The Opry thought Chet was a little too jazzy for them but Grandpa Ezra said, "Well, the Carters won't be there either. You take the whole kit and caboodle or you don't get anything."

LAURA CASH: And so they got uninvited to the Opry. Ezra said, "Well I'm sorry, but that's just the way it is." And he wasn't gonna back down. And so, a little while later, they called him again and raised the money. They said, "We'll give you such and such an amount of money," — and it was more than the first offer — "to come. But leave Chester at home." And Ezra stood his ground and said, "Absolutely not. He is part of this band."

I mean, we're talking about the Grand Ole Opry! And a contract, playing every weekend! He wasn't gonna do it without Chester. And finally, the Opry made room for Chester. And look at what he did for Nashville. He created the Nashville sound as a producer in the fifties. And, Nashville would never be the same without Chet Atkins.

LORRIE BENNETT: My mother never wanted to leave the family. She wanted to work with her family. Family was very important to her and she chose to stay with the family and didn't want to take that step out, to go out on her own. With the family — that was her place to be and that's what she enjoyed the most. I think she was ahead of her time as far as her voice was concerned. But I don't know that it was quite time for her to have stepped out anyway.

I think she did get a lot of respect for her talent. Everyone in the music business anyway knew what she was capable of doing.

Aunt Helen and Mom and Aunt June really never raised their voices. But Grandma and Aunt Helen argued like sisters. They argued all the time. We'd be in the car on the road going somewhere and they would be into it like sisters. I couldn't believe it. I guess it was because Grandma was so young when Helen was born. Maybe they kind of grew up together. That's all I can figure. But they argued all the time. Not serious things, silly things. "You know you're supposed to go this way!" "No, you should have gone that way." But generally speaking, they were all just laid back and calm and sweet-mannered, just great, sweet people.

JOHN CARTER CASH: Years after, when the Original Carter Family had disbanded, Maybelle Carter and the Carter Sisters went on the road and began singing these songs, throughout the fifties and the sixties and the seventies and the eighties and the nineties. Either Maybelle or — after Maybelle passed — the Carter Sisters continued to sing these Carter songs for hundreds and thousands and millions of people. The lasting influence of the Carter Family owes itself in a great part to the Carter girls and, of course, you know, to Maybelle after the Original Carter Family, for the simple fact that, in live performance, they sang to a lot more people than the Original Carter Family ever did. It was the Carter girls that carried that on. And, I believe that's one of the reasons why some of these songs are still so strong in our musical canon today. "Will the Circle Be Unbroken" was sung at the end of every Johnny Cash show from the early 1960's until he retired in 1997. And there are a lot of people that heard that in a live show. So, the legacy of the Carter Family, I believe, is a result of what the Carter girls did.

June Carter and Johnny Cash

Chapter Eight — John and June

The young boy from Dyess, Arkansas whose ear was pressed to the radio, tuning into the sounds of the Carter Family from the Mexican border, grew up to be their biggest fan. Later, fate would bring the Sun Records' artist in closer proximity to the Carters, altering his life and theirs irrevocably.

JOHNNY CASH: I met June Carter backstage at the Grand Ole Opry in 1956. That night, I told her, I said, "I'm gonna marry you someday." But neither one of us really took me seriously at the time. We were both with somebody else. But as time went on, it was 1961 before we ever worked together and 1962 before we really started on the road together as a team.

So from 1962, until June died this year (2003), we were together always, forty-one years. It's like a piece of me is gone out there somewhere, you know. But I won't go into that. That's a whole other life.

But in '63 or '64, I asked June to bring her family on the road. And she brought Mother Maybelle, Helen and Anita. So I had the whole Carter family clan there on the show with me. And we toured together all over the United States, Canada and Europe.

Life on the road with the Carter Family made it a pleasure to tour, believe me. The ladies were ladies. They were wonderful people, and I loved them all. I loved every one of them. 'Course I fell in love with that June, that red-headed one, that dancer, the one that told the jokes, the funny one. She stole my heart right away, right away. And I kept telling her, beginning then in '62, that "We're gonna get married. We've got to. You're meant to be mine. I know you are." I just knew it. And we fought to stay together. We fought people. We fought press. We fought everybody that tried to break us apart. Then in '68, we found ourselves both single. So we got married, March 1st, 1968. And we were together until she died. And we were two peas in a pod. We were never apart. June and I were never apart.

I wish everybody could have what we had because it's a wonderful thing. And you can't chalk it up to righteous living, because I was anything but righteous. I don't know. God richly blessed me for some reason. For some unknown reason, he richly blessed me with everything I ever wanted.

JOHN CARTER CASH — June Carter & Johnny Cash's Son: I think, when my father began to work with Maybelle and the Carter girls, that he was attracted to them because of their music. He was attracted to them because of the history of the music that he had grown up with, that he'd listened to his whole life. I think when he met them and began to spend time with them, what he found were people of his own kind. He found people that were connected to him directly in a matter of heart. They were of the same heart. And I've found letters that my father had written to my grandfather Ezra, and likewise my grandfather back to him, back and forth in the 1960's before he and June, my mother, were ever together.

He had a great love of knowledge, my dad did. And so did Ezra. They both loved books. There was a connection there that was very heartfelt. I think to them the music was all very important. But it was people. It was the fact that they were of the same kind. And that's what brought my father close to the Carters and why he stayed with them. They were of one family. And that can't be faked. And you can get up on stage and you can play with somebody year after year. The audience will know if it's real or not. Or they'll know if someone's just a backing musician.

Before my mother and father were ever married, they were family together. And the audience knew that. The audience heard that in the music. And they saw that in the spirit that was captured between my mother and father, of course. But the whole family, the whole Carter Family, was close to my dad in heart.

My father began working with my mother while he was still married to Vivian, his first wife. And my mother was married also. You know, it was a completely professional relationship. I think they became dear friends.

I think that it was inevitable that my father's first marriage fell apart. He was in turmoil. He was in pain and struggling. Some people say that it was my mother's love that saved him, or turned around or changed his life. I think if he hadn't changed, he would have died. And I think it was the fear of that in him, more than anything. But when you're at that point of your life, and someone is there that loves you and you love, that person is invaluable. And that person was my mother to my dad. And you know, their love for each other was longstanding, I'm sure, before they got married. But you know, when they did marry, and when they were together, my father, his life turned around. His life changed.

And my dad came back and found his spiritual roots.

This was due to the people who supported him and loved him — of course, my mother. But also, my mother's father, Ezra, and Maybelle and the other members of the Carter Family. It was that family unity that mattered so much.

<u>FERN SALYER</u> — Carter Sisters' Cousin:
June brought John to the valley while she was on the road with him. She wanted to show him the valley and have him meet her people and have him come see her Uncle Grant who was pretty sick at the time.

They were playing that night in Lebanon — Johnny and June were — and I know we went to the show. And that's the first time I ever really met him.

I thought June was crazy. Oh, he was nice. He was so mannerly and everything. And June would say, "He's such a good man if he can just get straightened out." And I thought, "June, you better wait till he get's straightened out!"

He would look at you, and you'd be almost intimidated because you felt like he not only was listening to you intently, he was looking into your soul. I thought, Gosh, what a man. He's almost more than a man.

We were close, and I loved him dearly. But the very day, even up until the day he died, I still had that strange feeling of not complete relaxation around him because of his intentness on what you were saying. I was scared he was analyzing everything I said. But he was some person. He was different like A.P. was different. They were talented people that had been sent here that we did not understand.

And he loved it here in Maces Springs. He called it home. And I said to him, "You've opened so many doors for us, things that we've seen and done that we'd never had seen, never done in our lives." I said, "For this whole valley, you have brought a lot of brightness into the valley," that we wouldn't have had without him.

Every time he came in, he'd go see my mom. I used to kid her. I'd say, "I think you fell in love with Johnny Cash." And you know, she was really sick then. She was bedfast. And she looked forward to him coming. And he'd go and sit and sing with her. And she would sing back with him. And he really liked my dad, too. He respected and loved older people. He had a lot of respect for them.

I remember hearing him talk about it. He said many times, "I think Maybelle was very instrumental in helping save my life." I don't think June could have handled that alone without some support from her family. At times she was about ready to give up.

But Maybelle being such a kind person, she knew that he was a special person. Like June used to say, "He's worth saving." And I'm sure Maybelle felt the same way. And she dearly loved that man. She loved him. She had no sons, so he was almost like a son. Maybelle wasn't like a mother to him, 'cause he loved his mother dearly. But Maybelle was a companion. She would go fishing with him. I think they had a very special relationship. I really do.

It was not lost on the Carters that Johnny Cash had a drug problem. It had destroyed his first marriage to Vivian Liberto, alienated friends and adversely affected his performances.

But the Carters did not judge him and rallied to help him get straight.

They went to the house he owned. They took him back there. And Maybelle and June moved in with him to help take care of him. And that's when they got Dr. Nat Winston to come in and help, too. And it was just a 'round the clock vigil with him. It had to be like going through hell and back to get through that ordeal. And even I've heard his brothers say he didn't think he was gonna make it at all, but he did. But I think June couldn't have done that alone. She couldn't have stood it, I don't think.

And I know Maybelle was there. Dr. Winston was there. And I'm sure his brothers and his sisters might have been there helping, too. But I think Maybelle was instrumental. She probably cooked him a lot of his favorite foods — she was a great cook.

RITA FORRESTER — June Carter's Cousin:
Of course, Johnny Cash came into our life when he met June. We were introduced to him before they married, sort of an old country custom where you meet someone's beloved before they actually get married. And you know, we grew up without a lot here. Certainly, in Nashville, they had a lot more money than what we have here. I remember being worried about what we would feed him. We went to the garden for vegetables to fix lunch. And he loved that and was so gracious and so good to us from the very first day we met him.

He adored Aunt Maybelle, June's mother. He loved June's sisters, I believe, almost as much as he loved June.

He loved all our family. He embraced June's entire family. We're a formidable family. I mean, we're a huge family for one thing. But he loved all of us right down to the cousins.

And I think he had a great appreciation for their place in history, for what they'd done. I think he thought it was ironic and really sort of sad that my granddad died probably never realizing the full impact of his work and what he had done. I think John always thought that was just terrible. And he wanted to make sure that people knew and remembered their place in history.

I know that he always thought it was awful that Aunt Maybelle had been on the road all her life, and worked all her life, and worked very hard. There was a time that she was sitting in the hospital as a nurse's aide. And he just thought it was horrible that she should have to do that and work that hard after she had worked so hard all of her life. But he was a big advocate of the Carter Family from the time he met them. He was a huge fan of their music.

He was such a commanding presence. He could be in the room and, even if you weren't aware you would know his presence was there. He was just so charismatic and so loving. And I guess that's the part of him that people who just saw him maybe in concert did not see. He had such a capacity for love.

We miss him so terribly. I mean, I can't tell you how much we miss him. It's hard.

I think he probably thought that the Carter Family sort of rescued him at a time in his life when he really needed rescuing. And they never backed down. And they never stopped loving him. Of course, you know, if you love someone you take them faults and all. And you don't stop loving

97

them. Of course, he appreciated that I think. We never gave up on him.

JOHN CARTER CASH: My father was on stage one night. And he turned around and looked at my mother and asked her if she would marry him — on stage in front of the audience. It didn't give her much of a chance to say no. You know, who knows how many times he might have asked her in the weeks before.

But gratefully, that time when he asked her on stage, she said yes. But he knew, I believe, that he would have many allies in his query. And the audience was on his side. They wanted to hear yes.

My mother knew Johnny Cash very well. I believe that when he asked her to marry him, she knew full and well that it was a dangerous proposition. She had been with him through some hard years. She'd seen his addiction. She'd seen his marriage fall apart with his first wife.

Of course, she saw that he loved her with all his heart and all his spirit honestly. And she loved him. And so that conquered all. That conquered her fear. At that point in my dad's life, he straightened up. He cleared up, and together they were strong for quite a few years.

My mother and father both sang songs of faith their whole life. Gospel was the most important music to my dad. If it hadn't been for gospel, he wouldn't have decided to go and try to be a professional singer. That's what he wanted to do.

Every show that my mother and my father did together, on the road together, they would sing gospel songs. And you know, they would mix the secular songs with the gospel music. And that format came from the Carter Family. It came from the fact that if you found a CD of twenty Carter songs there were gonna be at least six or seven of them that were gospel songs.

And you know, my dad took that; he felt comfortable doing the same thing in his work, because he'd seen them do it before him. That came, originally, from the Carter Family.

My father owned a cave near Chattanooga called Nickajack Cave. And he was lost and scared, alone. I think he was very, extremely depressed. I think he wandered into that cave with no thought of what he was doing and where he was going. It was daylight when he went in, so there was a little light in the area. But then it got dark.

He said that he got lost in that cave that night. And he prayed, God, get me out and I'll change my life. Perhaps that story is a bit allegorical. But I always heard it as being a true fact.

JOHNNY CASH: From day one that the Carter Family came on the road with me in '63, Mother Maybelle Carter was like the patron saint for all of us. Everybody respected her, loved her, adhered to her, tried to please her, tried to make her happy, comfortable — because she was Maybelle Carter. She was the most VIP that we've ever had on the road with us. And I have seen them all. I've seen them all, every one. But Maybelle Carter was the greatest star that I've ever known — without being a star, without trying to be a star, without even wanting to be a star.

She didn't want to be a star. She wanted to pick up a guitar. She wanted to go fishing with me. We did a lot of fishing together. She'd come over here, and we'd go down to the boat dock just cast a few times, and we'd always catch them. Or she would catch them. I'd watch her catch them, because she was a great fisherman. Or we'd go to Florida, to their house down there, to Maybelle and her husband Ezra's house in Florida. And we'd go out fishing in the Gulf of Mexico. And she'd yank them in all day long. Even I could catch them there though, because fishing was really good. But we didn't talk much. We didn't talk much at all.

I would get her to talking sometimes about the early days, like the days when she was on the road with Jimmie Rodgers or recording with Jimmie Rodgers. She would talk about it. She would open up to me. After awhile, she learned that it was all right to open up to me. Then she did. We became best buddies, and we talked about everything.

This kind of relationship continued until she died in 1978. Those are precious years to me. She was so important to me in my life. She taught me so much about life and about living. And she passed it all on to June. And then June had taken her own thing — June became June and Maybelle, you know. She picked up all those songs from her mother and she continued to sing them. Until the day she died, she was singing Carter Family songs. The old Clinch Mountain songs, the old valley songs, the old songs from the hills from Appalachian, the old down and out songs, lost love songs, everyone of them she sang. She sang to me.

CARLENE CARTER — June Carter's Daughter:
My Momma was a tomboy. But the thing about her is that she had this ambition in her. She was interested in much more than the valley. She loved the valley but she was interested in New York. She was interested in England. She

wanted to know about other places in the world. And she wanted to be an actress. She wanted to be an entertainer. She wasn't content to try and be a singer, because she didn't think she was a very good singer. So she found a way to entertain, and that was through her comedy and her personality. And the thing is, is Momma doesn't get much credit as she deserves for her comedy and for her singing and for her songwriting. I think people forget that she had a real good sense about writing songs. She was good at putting it all together.

She could be feeling really tired and worn out. And you know, particularly later on, as she got a little bit older . . . I'm talking about like, you know, in her sixties. But soon as it was time to go on stage, it did not matter. She was on, like a house on fire. She was on and glowing and it was like there was nothing to it.

My mother never met a stranger. Not ever. Rosanne tells the story about her answering the phone and talking for about thirty minutes. And someone saying, "Who was that?" And she says, "Oh, it was a wrong number." That was my mother. I swear, she just never met a stranger. And she was like that in her childhood too. And I think that's what endeared her to people in her life, period.

I think she always appreciated where she came from, because it helped her appreciate where she ended up.

My mother studied with Sandy Meisner in New York at the Neighborhood Playhouse. She very much wanted to be an actress. She'd take my little sister, Rosey, and me to New York at least twice a year. We'd go see Broadway shows — a lot of musicals. And it actually made me want to do that when I grew up. That was what I thought I wanted to be, a

101

Broadway actress in a musical. So I could tap dance and act and sing. And that's what I thought I wanted to do. And actually, as it turned out, I actually got to do that in my life, so that was kind of cool. But that's what my mother wanted to do. She wanted to be a dramatic actress as well. But she just never had many opportunities as I think she should have had.

When she married John there was a certain amount of not enough time for that stuff, in the beginning, because she was busy being married and busy being Johnny's partner. But later in life, she got to do some of that, which I know really, really meant a lot to her.

I did a show in the West End in London for a year. And my mother came over at least every three months, and would stay there for a week and come to every show. She was living a little bit vicariously through me in that regard, because I know she would have liked to have done that.

<u>LAURA CASH</u> — Maybelle Carter's Daughter-in-Law:
From what I understand, June really thought that acting was the place to be. She really wanted to be an actress. And she went to New York to go to school. And she met Robert Duvall in New York as children. "Bobby" Duvall was actually what she lovingly referred to him as.

And she did put in a lot of time. And there's photographs of her during that time. And she was so poised and beautiful and refined looking. And she really took a lot of pride in her acting roles.

<u>ROSANNE CASH</u> — Musician and Carter Family In-Law:
In the '60s, June used to do this bit in the show where she

would kick off her shoe, and it would appear to be accidental. But she would kick her leg really high and her shoe would go flying through the air. Then she'd have to kind of go out in the audience or wherever she'd kicked it and find it. And what was great is she'd be wearing this very beautiful dress. But then she would lift her skirts to go find the shoes and she had on these massive petticoats. So it was this great, beautiful, worldly, modern woman and you lift up and there's a mountain girl underneath. It was very funny. And she was funny.

She had this character called Aunt Polly that she had done long before she and my dad were together. Well, at one point, she finished with the character or Aunt Polly, and she actually buried her. She actually buried the costume, hat and everything, had a funeral for Aunt Polly and said, I will never do Aunt Polly again. She's done. Well, my dad had never seen Aunt Polly, but he had heard about her. So he kept pressing June, regularly for years and years. "Please do Aunt Polly. Please, please can I see Aunt Polly." "No, John. She's buried. I buried her, John. She's gone." Years went by with him continually pressing her. Well, one year, on his birthday, she had decided he had asked long enough, you know, ten years, twenty years, however long it was, that she was going to bring Aunt Polly back from the grave. And we had put on this little show for him for his birthday, with music and humor and all kinds of stuff. And suddenly Aunt Polly came out on the stage. My dad's jaw hit his knees. He was just transfixed through the whole thing. And Aunt Polly, not only was it funny but it was scary because June disappeared into Aunt Polly, this very funny mountain character that pre-dated Minnie Pearl, you know just as funny and kind of jarring. So my dad was thrilled to see Aunt Polly. So then of course, Aunt Polly had to go on the road with him. So during these shows, for the next couple of years, June had to do Aunt Polly. Then she said, enough. Aunt Polly is over with.

CARLENE CARTER: Rosanne and Rosey and Cathy and Cindy and Tara — we were all together as we could be. And there never was anything about being a stepsister at all, ever. It was just, "Those are my sisters. They always will be my sisters." That's how we were brought up.

At some point in there, me and Rosanne and Rosey got thrown on the stage together, all three of us. Rosanne and Rosey actually worked with them more on the road than I did, because I left home at fifteen and got married 'cause I got pregnant. So I didn't get to be on the road as much.

But after my daughter was a couple years old, I did go back on the road with them. And it was a way for me to start practicing my craft as a songwriter. And I just remember Rosanne and me and Rosey all sitting around and playing the guitars and being on fire. And being in the bus with John teaching us songs that he had learned off other artists that we'd never heard of. It was really, really exciting and inspiring and fun. And the three of us slept in one hotel room. We had a great time. And it was a wonderful time to be out there, too, watching his success and him and mom so in love. And John Carter being a baby, it was just sweet stuff.

When John and my Momma got together, to me it was a working relationship, because I was six years old when they started working together. So Momma worked with Johnny Cash, who we knew. And he was nice. But he couldn't come to our house because he was messed up. But we didn't know he was messed up. 'Cause you're a little kid, you don't even know what that means. I just remember Momma saying, "He's just a little funny. He can't come around here right now." But we would go on the road, and we were around him. But at the time, Momma was married to Rip, to Rosey's father. And I'm certain that John and June's relationship started when they started being on the road together. I'm positive of it, if it didn't start before then. But I remember her saying, "I'm gonna do this because I'm only gonna have to be gone ten days a month." That never worked out, but that was the plan.

I don't honestly remember a whole lot about Mom and Rip's relationship as a husband and wife. It never seemed to me that they were a mom and daddy unit. Rip was our Daddy Rip. And there was Momma. And Momma was on the road with John. But then when I turned ten, mom took me and Rosey to New York for one of our trips to see a show and sat us down and told us that Rip wasn't gonna be there anymore. And it was kind of brutal, but I don't think she knew how to tell us. And John was still married to Vivian. But June was free from Rip. And we started spending more time with John. He got to come to the house on my tenth birthday. He got to come to the house, and he bought me my favorite pair of roller skates that I'd been saving up for which cost forty dollars. Oh, my God. I'd been saving up and he bought them for me. And then, a few months later, he bought me my first electric guitar.

Anyway, we started spending a lot of time with him then. And me and Rosanne were twelve when John and June got married. And Mom sat me and Rosey down and said, "John and I are thinking about getting married."

By this point, we'd been going on vacations with him and always on the road with him. And his daughters had been coming to visit. So when Mom said John and I have decided to get married, Rosey and I said, "Well, when?" And she said, "But we're not going to if it's not okay with you guys," with me and Rosey. Ah! Like, that was gonna stop them. But you know, it was like playing lip service to us to make us feel important, whatever. So we had a little conference in the bathroom, me and Rosey did. And we came out and said, "It's okay," like we had all the power. "Well, when?" And Mom said, "Well, we're gonna wait till you guys get out of school in the summer." And we said, "Why don't you just do it now? We don't mind changing schools." And we just wanted Momma to be happy. And she was happy with John. So, they got married the next week.

So me and Rosey were kind of responsible for getting them to Kentucky to get married. And we were at the wedding with her friend, Miki Brooks. And Merle Kilgore was best man. And then there's little me and Rosey with our little outfits on. And they got married, and we moved to Hendersonville. And our lives drastically changed.

Mom was persnickety. She was kind of obsessed. She had a little OCD in certain areas. One of them had to do with mowing the yard. And we had fifteen acres. And we mowed the entire thing. And we had a little cart behind the riding mower. I mowed the whole yard and hand clipped all the fence rows, and had a garden and everything. That's all me and Rosey did, all the time.

So when Momma married John, we just thought that would just carry on so we could get our dollar a week allowance. And all of a sudden we couldn't, because of these fans hanging all over the fence and the gate. And you couldn't have the kids out there mowing the yard and clipping the hedgerows.

So suddenly, our allowance went up to ten dollars. And we suddenly couldn't mow the yard, which we didn't really know what do with ourselves, honestly. We were kind of like, wow! We thought we were supposed to get up in the mornings and do all these chores, and do everything to keep everything perfect.

Everything changed. We suddenly had a maid that did stuff. We weren't used to that. We had been brought up like Momma was in the valley up until she married John. And then it just didn't look right for us to be doing all this stuff. So everything kind of changed.

RANDY SCRUGGS — Musician:
For me, June Carter was family. Whenever I would think of June, I would think of Johnny and vice versa. They were so important for each other, throughout their time together. And it was so genuine. You could tell that, when she would speak of him, it was coming from a loving wife and partner. There was such love but also tremendous respect for each other. It was always so uplifting to see that and so inspiring.

I know, early on — this really goes back — my brother Gary and I recorded an album called *Scruggs Brothers*. This was our first album. We hadn't really even played performances yet. And this was in the late '60s. And at the time, Johnny Cash had *The Johnny Cash Show*, which was a really amazing network show at the time. He had artists like Bob Dylan come on, when Dylan wasn't doing live performances. It was filmed at the Ryman Auditorium here in Nashville.

But I think we bumped into June somewhere at that time. The next day, John's people called and said, "Can you come to the next taping?" We said, "You're kidding me? Okay, we'll definitely come down." So we were one of the guests that next night on his show. But both him and June were always that way. They had this perspective on things — they were interested in great musicians but also from young artists, too.

Always around them there would be somebody like Kris Kristofferson or Larry Gatlin — new kids on the block then. John and June had radar for finding someone who really was going to bring something fresh and amazing to the table. So you know, those remembrances are just tremendous for me.

About two weeks before June went in the hospital and passed away, I was at their cabin. I'd been doing some recording with John on his last few projects. And we had just finished this track. And June came in and said, "I really want to play you something." And it was the new album, the *Wildwood Flower*. At that time, it had not been released. So we just all sat there and listened to the album. And for me it brought back such memories of the influence they've had on me. It was also nice to see their son, John Carter, putting that project together.

It was something I'll never forget.

June Carter Cash died of complications following heart valve replacement surgery on May 15, 2003. Johnny Cash died on September 12, 2003 of complications from diabetes.

A.P. Carter's Grave

Chapter Nine — Twilight Years

CHARLES WOLFE — music historian and author:
After their Border Radio years, A.P. went back to Maces Springs. Sara went back to California. But A.P. couldn't quite get music out of his blood. He kept trying to do things. He wrote a book about the Bible, and he would go around to local radio stations and buy some time and sing a few songs and try and sell copies of that book. And as late as the early 1950's he was still doing that.

RITA FORRESTER — A.P. and Sara Carter's Granddaughter:
After my grandmother left, my granddad obviously had his children to raise which was unheard of for a man in that day and time to do. He still had some things that he did with music. He didn't do as much with his music but he still performed some and he was still very much interested in music. But once his children were grown, his life was somewhat empty, I think.

He did date other women although it was brief and I guess he thought about remarrying but he always said that he was afraid that whomever he would marry would not be good to his children and he couldn't bear it if they weren't.

So he had a lot of friends but he never married any of them and basically lived with his children. He stayed with us until just before he got really sick at the end of his life.

He was very active with the grandkids. He loved his grandchildren. That kept him busy. He built the little store – — which is now a museum — and he ran it. He would stay in it a lot. He had his little bed in there that he kept and people would come visit him in the store and he would play music there.

We always had lots of visitors from the time I was little. They would come at least once a week we'd have visitors and it was all about the music that they were coming for.

And I grew up thinking that everybody had that many visitors, that every family had carloads of people that they didn't know that came to see them. And I think he filled his life up with things but he probably had a very lonely time for a while.

But he loved his kids and his grandkids so that kept him very busy. He was surrounded with a lot of love, certainly.

FLO WOLFE — A.P. and Sara Carter's Granddaughter:
After A.P. and Sara and Maybelle quit doing their thing sometimes A.P. would have pickup bands that go out and do shows. And back then all we had was the fireplace and the house was cold and when you started to bed you got your flannel blanket and stood in front of the fireplace, got just as hot as you could wrapped up in that blanket and got into bed and pulled the covers up till you got your bed warm.

So A.P. would come in at 2 or 3 o'clock in the morning after going out and playing. There'd be all these people who we didn't know and I had to give up my bed — my good warm bed — to somebody I didn't know and seems like I've always resented that. I usually slept downstairs. I had to give my bed to a bunch of musicians I didn't know.

<u>RITA FORRESTER</u>: There were people seeking him out. And they did that as long as I can remember. People who knew his history. He saw the very beginnings of the revival of folk music in 1960. There were people though, even before then, who knew what he had done and appreciated his contributions. Bill Clifton was one of them. The Seegers definitely realized that.

As a young man growing up in Maryland, Bill Clifton developed a passion for the Carter Family's music, collecting their records and dreaming of a day when he might meet A.P Carter. Eventually, he became a musician himself, forming a bluegrass group called the Dixie Mountain Boys. He finally met A.P. Carter in 1950 and came to feel that A.P. Carter was like a second father to him. But meeting his idol almost didn't happen.

<u>BILL CLIFTON</u> — Musician/Carter Family Friend:
One day I went into my local record store and asked, "Why aren't you getting any more Carter Family records?" And the owner said, "Well, I don't know." I said, "Can you find out?" And he said, "I'll ask the RCA man next time he's in." So, a couple of weeks later I came in again. "Did you ask the RCA man why you aren't getting any Carter Family records?" And the owner said, "Yeah, they think the old man died" meaning A.P. I was just heartbroken. I thought, "I'll never, ever get to meet A.P. Carter." Of course, I was interested in meeting Sara and Maybelle, too. But I was particularly interested in A.P. I just had a feeling about him. I really liked this man. And I loved the music. And I had a feeling that he was responsible for a lot of what they did. So for a couple of years I thought he was dead. And then when I was an undergradu-

ate student at the University of Virginia, my first year, I didn't have any classes at noon and I listened to a program from WFLO in Farmville, Virginia, that Bill and Mary Reed did at noon every day. And I was listening to it one day and Bill Reed came on and said, "Don't touch that dial. I don't know what you're doing, but don't touch that dial. Stay right where you are. You won't believe who just walked in the studio. But, we're gonna introduce him to ya after our first song. And, don't go away 'cause you're gonna want to meet this man and hear him."

And so I thought, "Well, it's somebody from the Grand Ole Opry stopped by. That's a big deal, maybe Hank Snow or somebody." So I stayed listening. And, then Bill Reed came on and he started in, "This gentleman, with his wife and sister-in-law . . ."

I just couldn't believe it. I thought, "There's nobody else . . . it couldn't be anybody else!" It was A.P. Carter! It just touched me.

And that was when I first discovered that A.P. Carter was alive, and I made it my next move to figure out how to find him and to get to him as soon as I could. And I think this happened in November. And it took me till April to get down to Maces Springs. By that time I was doing a morning broadcast myself on the local radio station, WINA in Charlottesville. So I was beginning to do semi-professional music, and I thought, "Well, I can introduce myself to him as somebody who is doing radio at least. So that gives me some credibility." And I went down to see him.

I knew what Maybelle's house looked like because Maybelle had put a songbook out with a picture of her house up against the mountain. And I thought if I get to Maces

Springs then I'll be able to find her house and I know he's close by. But I found him before that because I came up the road and I approached this building, and I saw a sign, A.P. Carter Groceries. And I thought, "I didn't know he ran a little grocery store," but I immediately stopped the car. But there was a lock on the door.

So I continued on up the road another hundred and fifty yards to where a man was mowing the grass. And I stopped the car and I got out. And he stopped his lawnmower. I said, "I just wonder if you could tell me where A.P. Carter lives?" And he pointed to the open door of the house. "He's sitting on the couch right there."

And I just walked in and introduced myself to A.P. Carter.

He was sitting there listening to the radio; he had a country music program on. I just came in and I stood for a moment. And he motioned for me to sit down. So I sat down next to him. He wanted to hear something on the radio and after he heard it he turned the radio off and I introduced myself and we began to talk. And I told him that I had a radio program and every day I always did a Carter Family song. And I guess being as young as I was — I was nineteen at the time — I guess I was one of the few people who he'd met who was that young, who was interested in their music. That's all I can think of. I don't know otherwise why he would have had the time of day for me. But, there weren't many young people interested in Carter Family music. And, quite honestly I noticed that most people had switched to electric guitar; that's where the money was. People in Nashville were making money. And they were playing electric instruments. So, people in the valley had already started to switch over. I guess he saw in me somebody who was continuing the acoustic tradition of the kind of music that his life was about.

We just got on beautifully and, always did, for ten years, all along. He lived ten years more. He was thirty-nine and a half years my senior. He was born December 15th. I was born April 5th. He was born in 1891 and I was born in 1931, so we had almost forty years difference. But we became really close friends.

A.P. kept trying to match me up with one of the girls in the valley. I think he thought if I married one of the girls that I would move here. I did move to Maces Springs, but I didn't marry a local girl though.

We'd sit on that porch outside the store for a little while, but he wouldn't sit there very long. We'd sit and talk for a little while and then he'd want to get up and do something else, walk somewhere. "Let's go up on the mountain and get a drink of water out of the stream up there."

He had long legs. And when I came up here, I'd been in the Marine Corps and I was in better shape than I've ever been in my life. I was twenty-three, twenty-four years old. And he would walk me up that mountain so fast that by the time I got up there I was exhausted. He had a lot of nervous energy. And that would show in his daily routines, no matter what he did. He didn't keep regular hours with the store, for example. If there was a lock on the door, people knew that, "Well, he'll be back later." And sometimes we'd come back from somewhere and there'd be five or six, seven people just standing around.

And I learned a lot about A.P. from just listening to that radio program. For example, after he finished his song, Bill and Mary Reed came back on and said, "Wait a minute Mr. Carter. Don't get your overcoat off the piano yet. We're gonna ask you to come back and do another song."

But A.P. was somebody who thought, "Well, I've just done it" and would just get up and leave. He was that kind of person, I found out over the years.

Same way that I discovered that he often sang bass for a little while, and then disappeared during recording sessions. I often wondered why, until we did a show at a radio station together. I was singing tenor, Johnny Clark [a fellow member of the Dixie Mountain Boys] was singing high baritone, and A.P. was singing lead, and right in the middle of the song A.P. just walked over to the window in the studio and started looking out. Johnny and I looked at each other, and A.P. was over looking out the window. So the lead singer was gone.

At that point in time, there was nothing happening for the Carter Family. Nothing at all. One time I saw a royalty check come in from Peer International or Southern Music. It was the first time I ever saw him get a check from Peer, I think it was a hundred and twenty-seven dollars. This was maybe 1952 or '53. Hundred and twenty-seven was more than a hundred and twenty-seven is today, but it still wasn't a lot of money considering they had over two hundred songs. But not much was being recorded.

And A.P said, "I need to get a couple of counter checks." So we went to the bank. And he got a check for one third of the money and made it out to Maybelle and one third and made it out to Sara and took the cash for the other third, and immediately put the checks in the mail to Sara and Maybelle. He could have easily just pocketed the money. It was sent to him, you know. But he was not that kind of person.

A.P. decided to build a music venue near the home place. He dubbed it Carter's Park.

Carter's Park was up on the hill. He had to rebuild the stage every year because it was just made for one summer season. But I used to come down from the Jamboree in Wheeling. On Saturday night, I worked in Wheeling and then I'd drive down after the Jamboree and play Sunday at the park. A.P. didn't have any fences. It was a dollar a person, unless you were under twelve years old. So, of course, a lot of people had big families and a lot of people were always there. A.P. paid a percentage of the gate to me. And sometimes, I'd look at the crowd. It's over a thousand people, and I'd get two hundred dollars. But I knew he was honest.

And, it was years later that A.P.'s grandson Dale, was talking to me about the park. Dale said, "I had some experiences that kind of told me a little bit about my grandpa." Dale said when he was about thirteen-years-old, one day a man hobbled over to the fence and he had only one leg. And he said, "Are you A.P. Carter's grandson?" And Dale said, "Yes, sir." He said, "You know, I used to go to the music up at Carter's Park and take my family up there. And, you know, he never would let me pay."

I said, "Dale, A.P. knew who could pay and who couldn't. He knew that that man didn't have the wherewithal to take care of his family. And he wanted everybody to have a chance to hear the music."

A.P. never quite gave up on the dream of reviving the act. In 1950, he and Sara along with their son Joe and daughter Janette made some recordings for a small label called Acme, owned by a Kentucky preacher. But distribution of these records was poor and very few people heard them. A few years later, the Original Carter Family — Sara, A.P. and Maybelle — performed at the first Jimmie Rodgers Memorial event in Meridian, Mississippi. It would be the last time they would play together. The event was captured on a crude recording.

JOHN CARTER CASH — Maybelle Carter's Grandson:
On this recording, A.P. seems so sad. He says, "Maybe you don't remember the Carter Family?" And it was almost as if he felt like he had to give a little education to the audience. And it may have been true. There may not have been many people that knew the Carter Family's music.

FLO WOLFE: It seemed like when he got old and ill, A.P. turned back to the music. I know one day he was feeling really, really bad and the record player was in the living room. We'd set up a bed for him in the dining room near the bathroom and he wanted to hear "Jealous Hearted Me." I don't know why that song. He wanted that played all day long just as loud as we could play it. I know Mother said, "Well, I don't know what the neighbors are going to think," and the people going up and down the road. But we played that over and over that day. It's just something he wanted to hear.

I know Bill Clifton and Bill's first wife came down to see

119

him. And A.P. wanted Bill to act like he was announcing music on the radio. He got senile. He sort of talked more about his music then than he did before he got sick. He sort of went back to it.

RITA FORRESTER: Toward the end, his mind was not very good and he thought he was back on border radio and he had my mom and Bill Clifton sing. He would think he was doing shows and they would humor him and sing. Whatever he wanted they did it.

I know one night they sang about all night long because he was in a different place.

He was a staunch Republican. And one of the things that he told me when I was little, that I always remember was, "Now sit on my knee. I have to tell you something that you just have to remember all of your life" and I thought, "Boy, this is gonna be good." I had to be about three-years-old. And I thought it was gonna be something about my soul and how I'm supposed to live my life. And he said that I was supposed to vote Republican. [*chuckles*]

When he passed all his family was with him, which is what you would expect. We even had the wake at the home place, in that day and time you didn't go to the funeral home. He was laid out in the living room. That's how they did things then and, of course, his service was at Mount Vernon and he wanted to be buried at Mount Vernon. But he died like he lived, surrounded by everyone that he loved.

I think my granddad was ahead of his time in so many ways. He wanted a particular type of headstone because he told his children, "You know, people will be coming to see my grave. And I want it to be different, unique and something that they remember."

I guess the one thing that's most important to me is that people realize that my granddad, was the driving force behind all of this and that without him and his driving vision there wouldn't have been a Carter Family and that the face of American music would be much different and not nearly as vast and encompassing as it is today.

He sacrificed a lot for that — for his dream and for his vision. He sacrificed his family basically, the love of his life and he gave a lot for that. But that's the most important thing to me that people realize what he sacrificed to do what he did and how much credit he deserves for preserving so much of our musical history and actually just laying the groundwork for it, laying the groundwork for country music and setting it out on the path that it's on today actually, making it a music about family, about the love of the Lord. He was a big part of that and it's important to me that people know what a big part he was. I guess that's the most important thing.

I feel like he probably never realized what he had done, and his contributions to music. He would have been bowled over by the fact that his face is on a postage stamp. He would have loved that. He would have got a kick out of that, probably even more so than getting into the Country Music Hall of Fame. See, he missed all of that. Aunt Maybelle and my grandmother lived to see that. But even if he had seen it, he would have been the same, down-to-earth basic country person that he was otherwise. He was just one of the greatest men I've ever known. If he had any faults I certainly never saw any of them.

JANETTE CARTER — A.P. Carter's Daughter:
Daddy moved in with me, where he was sick and in bad health. The last three years of his life was here at this house. Days before he died, I was in bed. And he said, "You come in here Janette. I want to talk to you."

And so I went in there. And he said, "I want to ask you something." He said, "I want you to promise me that my music will be carried on." And I said, "Daddy, how in the world am I gonna do it, I don't know. I've got little children I'm trying to raise. But I will try."

And I said, "I'll never do nothing that brings dishonor to my people, or to you."

So I made two vows. And I've kept them both.

Chapter Ten — Not Forgotten

A.P. Carter's death on November 7, 1960 went largely unremarked in the media and the Original Carter Family's contributions faded into the background of a burgeoning American popular music scene.

However, Maybelle and the Carter Sisters had enjoyed considerable success in the years since the Carter Family breakup. Touring with Johnny Cash had given them additional visibility. But changes in the Carter sisters' personal lives sometimes sidelined Maybelle. The sisters were having babies, raising families and doing their own recording projects. For a while Maybelle worked as a nurse's aide to fill her free time. Meanwhile, Sara continued to live a quiet life in California.

Fortunately, new generations of musicians began to discover these pioneering musicians, among them a group of folk musicians called the New Lost City Ramblers.

<u>MIKE SEEGER</u> — Musician:
The New Lost City Ramblers got together as just a happening. It was just an informal meeting on a radio program. We were guesting. And I'd kind of broken into what was basically a John Cohen and Tom Paley radio show, and it seemed to work a little bit. I played the fiddle. And nobody in the city

was playing fiddle with this kind of music. They're playing banjo and guitar, maybe a little mandolin, so that made it different. And John, Tom and I shared a love for old-time music and singing.

Maybelle Carter

So after a while, it looked like we could get a few gigs, and we did. And shortly after that, within a couple of years, we were singing the Carter Family songs because John could sing bass a little bit, like A.P., and we loved their songs and their singing.

Soon after we got started, we began doing concerts with traditional artists. It seemed like the natural thing to do, not only to bring the music through us but also to bring the people we learned from to urban audiences. Our first was Elizabeth Cotten, and then Roscoe Holcomb and Dock Boggs.

Out in the West Coast there was a place called the Ash Grove in Hollywood. And we kind of worked with them to bring traditional musicians to the West Coast. And in 1963 one of those musicians was Maybelle Carter.

It was an amazing, wonderful honor. She was double booked the first two or three days. So she sent a substitute in, and that was Johnny Cash. And Johnny played opening act for us.

After that we traveled with Maybelle. I don't think I ever talked with Maybelle about what her anticipation was for this tour. I had a feeling that she took everything as it came. And in fact, we went to pick her up at Los Angeles Airport and saw that precious L5 Gibson guitar come down the baggage chute! We kept it from hitting the edge of the carousel.

We said, "We'd like to go rehearse now." But this was in the early morning — she'd been on a flight from gosh knows where, and she was tired.

And after about an hour of rehearsal, which we didn't entirely need because we knew her songs pretty well, she said, "Boys, I'm a little tired. I'd like to go and rest." And so I

125

remember, we were kind of sheepish about it — asking this great heroine of ours to rehearse when she was tired.

We backed her up with bass and guitar. She hadn't done much of that on her own. She'd been with her daughters and maybe another musician or so. And she wasn't entirely used to it. But she got used to it. And she got used to talking to people about the kinds of things that we were interested in, because that's what we were talking with her about backstage. People would bring in records for her to autograph. And her fans would come in from around the Los Angeles area. So we'd share her with her fans.

And then we drove to Tucson for a concert to which I think a half a dozen people came. And she regaled us with stories of Nashville artists that were flipping out that she had helped through the night by just going and talking with them. They'd call her up in the middle of the night saying, "Mama, I need to talk." People that you know well like Johnny Cash. She was an amazingly solid person who helped all kinds of people.

I hesitate to use the word "humble" to describe her because she wasn't humble. She was very solid but understated.

She was a good storyteller. And there was continuity to what she would say, continuity and lots of feeling, but very understated and matter of fact in a way. She seemed to take life as it came.

And she was absolutely dignified, both she and Sara.

My friend Ed Kahn and I went to visit up in Angel's Camp where Sara lived and had a wonderful day of talking and seeing Maybelle and Sara together at home in their very close friendship.

It was absolutely amazing when we recorded Sara and Maybelle. We were just sitting around in Sara's mobile home and they were trying to find songs that they could do and they were going through song after song after song and they managed to get through "I'm Leaving You." Maybelle was so fluent on the guitar at that time. To be able to play that piece with a flat pick when she'd been playing most everything for the previous couple of weeks with her fingers and thumb and finger pick. It was amazing.

And then since it's in the key of F, which is not an easy key on the guitar, and she was playing B flat while she was warming up for it, she not only played the B flat down close to the end of the guitar, she played one where she barred up on the sixth fret. She just loved to do that. She was proud in a very quiet way. It was very charming to see.

She'd do something very flashy and just go on. I knew what she was doing. She knew I was watching her — because I was. [chuckles]

Maybelle was the experimenter. She was the progressive. She was always looking for something to do and she was reaching outside of country music for things because she loved different kinds of music, including Hawaiian music and black music.

I was always intrigued with how Maybelle chose a rhythm guitar made for jazz players to play. A friend of mine said, "Well, that's because it was the most expensive guitar that they made then," which could have been the reason for her and Eck to get that. But also in retrospect, in those mellow recordings it's the only guitar which really would cut as well as that guitar needed to cut — to stand out — with the two guitars. Sara would play a very laidback

127

guitar with no finger picks and then Maybelle would have this almost macho guitar [*chuckles*] which really cuts. It has a very assertive tone, I guess you'd say, a more brittle tone.

Sara was much more remote than Maybelle. Maybe "remote" is a little harsh. The word doesn't come right now. I think she didn't want to express some of those feelings, and for what reason I don't know. But I wouldn't characterize her as an emotional singer. She was a wonderful, wonderful singer. But I wouldn't say that emotional outbursts in the singing were part of it.

I don't know how to characterize her personality any better. To me, she felt like a woman of substance but you couldn't quite get at it. The substance came out in her singing. And it came out in other ways too when she would talk.

It's just an old-time way of dealing with emotional issues. She wasn't "yer little old mountain woman." She certainly was not that, nor was Maybelle.

The Carters were giants of people. These were people who had their own special sophistication and value which was so exceptional that the three of them made music that's still compelling to us seventy some years later.

The New Lost City Ramblers were not the only group that came to appreciate the Carter legacy. In California in the late '60s, a young band named the Nitty Gritty Dirt Band embraced this roots music and used it to build an important cultural bridge with their 1972 album, Will the Circle Be Unbroken. *This recording included many music greats of the era, including Maybelle Carter.*

JEFF HANNA — Musician, Nitty Gritty Dirt Band:

Growing up in Southern California, most of our band were surfers but we didn't really like surf music, except for Dick Dale and the Deltones which was pretty cool. We were all little folk puppies. We were all guys that got exposed to this music through the more commercial end of it like the Kingston Trio and Peter, Paul and Mary and stuff like that and we'd read the liner notes to see where these songs came from and so worked backwards from there.

And we saw the Carter Family name on a lot of stuff. I remember having an LP — a Pete Seeger instruction course on how to play folk guitar — and there was a thing on how to learn the Carter scratch which combines rhythm and melody. But that got us into the songs and if you were to interview any of the guys in our band they'd tell you the same thing. Before there was a Dirt Band we all kinda knew about the Carter Family.

And as time went on and we got deeper into the music we heard other folks like Flatt and Scruggs or Doc Watson doing Carter Family material and it was like, "Wow, who are those people and where did they come from and where did this music come from?" And it seemed so far away and so exotic to us. We were out there on the West Coast and we wondered about places like West Virginia and Tennessee and Virginia and it was like, "Wow, we need to go there" [*chuckles*] and actually we did.

Of course we were all huge Flatt and Scruggs fans and we played a concert at Vanderbilt University in Nashville back in, I believe, 1970 and we had a record out called *Uncle Charlie and His Dog Teddy* that had "Mr. Bojangles" on it which was a big hit at that point. And we did this concert and

129

found out that Earl Scruggs and his family were coming to the show which made us really excited and really nervous.

RANDY SCRUGGS - Musician, Carter & Cash Family Friend: A lot of times, if there was a certain artist coming to town, I might go to the concert, say, with my brothers. But the Dirt Band was playing Vanderbilt University here in Nashville, and I'd heard about them. I knew some of their records. But I knew that they also blended not only forms of pop music at that time, but also had fiddle, mandolin and banjo as instrumentation.

So anyway, I mentioned to the rest of my family that they were playing there. And we ended up all going to the concert. And later at the end of the concert we went backstage and met them. And then they knew just everything about my dad's music and his background, and knew that my brothers and I were starting to work with him in part of this new band, the Earl Scruggs Revue. So we immediately became great friends and started to do some tours together. But also a few months after that we played in a club in Boulder, Colorado called Tulagi. Several of the Dirt Band lived in the Boulder area. So they came to our concert there.

And later on, we went back to the hotel and started playing, just jamming and stuff. And through our conversation that evening with my Dad and John McEuen, there was a discussion about wouldn't it be great to go to Nashville and maybe record with some legendary figures or artists of the time. And I think Dad said, "Well, if you are serious about it, then let's do it." And John's brother, Bill McEuen, was the person who produced *Will The Circle Be Unbroken, Volume 1.* So he basically made the arrangements, and they had a very

130

limited budget. And they thought they'd be here for just two or three days recording ten songs or some kind of deal like that.

My dad has always been interested in other forms of music and different artists. He just loves great music whether it's pure bluegrass or country or rock or whatever. The Dirt Band guys had said something about maybe Roy Acuff being involved and asked my dad if he had any ideas about some other artists. So in their discussions, Dad was able to go to give them his recommendations. And he basically let the legendary artists he approached know that the Dirt Band guys were great musicians and that they were really serious about this project. They were not coming here to try to change something so much as wanting to capture part of it and be part of it.

<u>JEFF HANNA</u> — Musician, Nitty Gritty Dirt Band:
It was really amazing with the Scruggs and the Cash and Carter families all really close — always have been — so, you know, Earl just made a call basically and asked her if Maybelle would like to be involved in this thing and she said, "Yes." So it was our gain in a huge way. It was great. I mean, finding out that we were gonna be able to meet Maybelle Carter was a really big deal. Part of the thing that happened with that *Circle* record was we were getting to meet these folks and hang out with them but also getting to play music and then record it with them. It looks great on your permanent record, you know? It was Christmas every day in the studio. There's a photo of us from that session that's on the inside artwork of the album and we're literally at her feet. [*chuckles*] What a presence. I mean amazingly

sweet, good natured, and all that talent, too. It was quite a combination.

She was a road warrior. She was a traveling, working musician in a world that was dominated by men, of course. So she had her ways of kinda hanging in there with the boys. She used to call us "them dirty boys" by the way. That's what June told us which I loved. She said, "You know Mama always called you guys 'them dirty boys.'" I thought that was the sweetest. [*chuckles*]

What Maybelle brought to the session aside from her wealth of talent was just this great sort of spiritual feeling which was great for us. Because we were operating on a combination of fear and excitement and joy all kinda bundled together during these sessions. Because we were thrilled that we were there but we were also scared to death that we better play okay and sing okay. But she was just so like, "Boys, it's no big deal." She just had this great, lovely presence about her.

I think what came out of those sessions was that there were these two gaps that were bridged, a generation gap because here we were guys that were not that far out of our teen years and working with older musicians who are younger than I am now, by the way [*chuckles*] and also the cultural gap. The Vietnam War was raging and there was this political division between people and it was peace marches and Nixon and the country was divided. Imagine that. [*chuckles*]

I know that there was a lot of explaining for the Scruggs family and for Mr. Acuff and for the Carters, you know, when people were saying, "Well, what are you doing making music with these scruffy dudes from the West Coast?"

And I think that, of course, the element that wiped out all of that misconception was the music. That was the common ground and I think something great that came out of that was it helped take away some of the prejudice on both sides.

RANDY SCRUGGS: Then they came to Nashville. And at that point, Dad was going to be on the album, Maybelle Carter, Roy Acuff, Doc Watson, Vassar Clements, several different artists. And once they started recording, I think it was just like they just couldn't stop. There was no way they could stop. They just had to keep going. They ended up recording three albums worth of material that all became part of *Will The Circle Be Unbroken Volume 1*. It was a triple album release.

And for me, it was a great experience because I was just out of high school. I personally knew all the people involved.

So I was just having fun. I was just there for the experience of it. But it turned out to be such an amazing piece of history. In a lot of ways, it was a turning point for some music that started happening around that time, where there was some coming together of rock — like the Byrds and their influences — and country music.

An interesting side note is that around the time that we were doing *Volume 1* of *Will the Circle be Unbroken* a lot started to happen with audiences and this music. There had been folk festivals before then and some rock festivals. But suddenly, festival attendance started to really grow and there was also a blend of musical talent that was playing. I know we would play and, sometimes it would be us and the Carter Family and the Dirt Band. But then, there might be

B.B. King and the Byrds, or just other bands and artists that were really making interesting music at that time.

Things went from being just a rock festival or just a bluegrass festival to simply being a music festival. It could be almost like Woodstock out in the country somewhere. But there could be seventeen or eighteen thousand people three nights in a row for all these performances. I think for Maybelle and the Carter sisters this probably was a bit of a surprise. But I think it exposed a really huge audience to some other music that they hadn't known before.

To us, it was like the early pickin' parties times ten thousand.

As was typical of the Carters, these festival performances became a multi-generational undertaking. Maybelle's grandchildren often toured and performed with her.

CARLENE CARTER — Maybelle Carter's Granddaughter:
And I remember myself and my sister Rosanne, and my little sister Rosey were playing a show with Grandma and Helen and Anita. They let us be part of the Carter Family. We were playing with the Nitty Gritty Dirt Band in Morgantown, West Virginia and it was a college crowd and this is right after the *Will the Circle Be Unbroken* album.

I always knew my grandma had it going on, you know. There was no question about that. It was just that I didn't realize the impact that she had had across the board to cause an audience of these pot-smoking college kids sitting cross-legged on the floor to suddenly stand up just when she walked on the stage. And she hadn't played a note yet.

It didn't really dawn on me till then that it was such a big deal because she was just my grandma and we hung out and we fished and we played poker and she gave me coffee that was all sugary and creamy when I was a little kid. She was like my pal and my buddy. And she played the guitar and I loved that part of it. And I wanted to do that and started really young because of her. And playing just happened to be her job.

But at that moment, I do remember going, "Oh, my goodness. There's something bigger here than what I realized."

With Grandma, it wasn't really a job. It was a large part of her existence as a walking, talking human being on this earth; she played guitar and she sang and that's what she loved to do.

I remember her telling me, "I'm going down there with these long haired boys. They sing pretty nice and I'm gonna make a record with them. For some reason they want me to play guitar on it." That naïve quality of hers. She said, "They seem like real nice young men." She was amazed that these young guys, who were "rock guys," were interested in playing with her.

She was surprised by the youth in the audience. As she was getting older, they were getting younger and younger and younger, and knowing who she was and what she'd been doing her whole life. That's pretty cool. She was happy about it, but was still thinking, "I don't understand why." She was cute about it.

Grandma just was kind of a sponge. And it's like nobody really taught her anything. She just kind of soaked it up.

135

And she did cross all kinds of genres. She did sing background on [the Johnny Cash song] "You Dirty Old Egg Sucking Dog." And probably sang it completely seriously.

There was a naivety about her that was so precious. She wanted to put [Brewer and Shipley's song] "One Toke Over the Line" in the Carter Family set because it said "One toke over the line, Sweet Jesus." She thought that that was a really good gospel song.

LORRIE BENNETT — Maybelle Carter's Granddaughter:
And we had to explain to her, "No grandma that won't work, that won't work." It was hilarious. She thought it was a catchy tune. She loved that song. "That's a really good song. I think we ought to do that on the next album." And we'd say "Grandma, honey, that won't work." I think mom even said it. Even mom realized it. [laughs] "No, honey, no. Yeah, it is a catchy song, it's a nice one, but we don't need to put that on our album." [*chuckle*] "That won't work for us".

CARLENE CARTER: But she liked all kinds of music. And I loved it that all kinds of other people, in different areas of music loved her music. When radio started segregating us musically, my grandmother crossed all those lines. I mean, Jerry Garcia held her in high acclaim, you know. Who would ever think that my grandma could possibly be a Dead Head? But I think she would have been. Her and Jerry would have probably jammed. Maybe they're jamming up in heaven.

LORRIE BENNETT: She was a very gentle soul. She was quiet and just very sweet. She never realized what impact she had on the music industry. And I probably didn't realize it, as much until I started working these bluegrass festivals with her. We had to walk through the crowd to get to the stage a lot of times. And these "long hair people" were out there and they just parted and made way like they were in awe. It was really quite touching. Nobody ever bothered any of us, everybody just stood back, just like she was a goddess, you know.

She just smiled like she always did. She was quiet. She was almost shy I think. I don't think she realized what it really meant to these people. There would be people at these festivals that would just strip down and be dancing and carrying on and her little eyes were kind of bugged anyway. And they would REALLY bug out when that started happening. But she never let on that it ever bothered her or anything. She just kept right on singing. That's what she always did.

But she could give you the gosh-awful-est looks if anybody hit a sour note or made a mistake. She wasn't going to hide it. She looked at you like, "What in the world have you done?"

But she was great.

CARLENE CARTER: I was pretty much on the road with Grandma and Helen and Anita because Mom was with John. And they would do these gigs as the Carter Family. And so we would drive twenty-two hours to do a show at a firemen's ball. And we'd play on the back of a flatbed truck. This is in the '70s. It was nothing to them to drive that far and to turn around and go back home another twenty-two hours. And Grandma always drove, she always felt like that's just part of it. And she always gave fans what they wanted. She'd always play, even when her hands started hurting, when she got arthritis. She just switched to playing autoharp a lot more than guitar, because she couldn't make her fingers do it exactly perfect anymore.

Somebody asked me not too long ago, "Who raised you?" You know that saying, it takes a village to raise a child? I had a whole family that raised me and they all raised each other's kids, too. We all grew up very much under the wings of Grandma and her girls leaning over us kids. It was a great, comfortable place to be.

Chapter Eleven — Returning to the Fold

During some of Maybelle's activity in the '60s and '70s, she was able to lure her old friend Sara from out of seclusion in California to take part. Still, Sara was not enamored with playing and appearances were few and far between.

RITA FORRESTER — A.P. and Sara Carter's Granddaughter: For the most part the end of my grandmother's life was not about music. She had pretty well left all that behind. She did some concerts in the '60s, some of the folk festivals — went to the Newport Folk Festival that sort of thing — but I don't think she ever really missed doing the music that much. She would do it and she had fun when she did it but I think she was happy to be private in the last part of her life.

And I think she was surprised, too, by some of the things that happened. Certainly the Carter Family's induction into the Country Music Hall of Fame, the things that she and Aunt Maybelle got to see. And she always loved to be around Aunt Maybelle. They were buddies to the very end and got very close to each other as a matter of fact, very close together.

But I imagine her life was even lonelier than my grand-dad's. Sadly, I imagine that's the case.

But Sara willingly agreed to take part in one special event in August of 1975 in Maces Springs. Hosted by her daughter Janette, the A.P Carter Memorial Day Festival would soon spawn an annual Carter Family Festival in addition to an ongoing weekly concert series at a venue that would come to be called the Carter Family Fold.

Janette Carter at the A.P. Carter Museum

FERN SALYER — Carter Sisters' Cousin:
Maybelle and Sara played at the first festival. I guess that was probably the first musical festival outside that I ever

went to. And I remember Helen being on stage and, of course, Janette and Joe and Sara and Maybelle. I thought it was great. I can't remember who the other entertainers were, but I remember they were there.

It was a big deal. Who would have the guts to even start something like that? You had to have a lot of tenacity about you to even start something like a festival in the middle of nothing.

But you know, a long time ago, A.P. had this in mind. He had a vision. And he had a stage in the mountain that he was gonna start making music.

JANETTE CARTER — A.P. and Sara Carter's Daughter:
You know music goes through different phases. The old-time music was just practically overshadowed by other music. At times, it was just about at the bottom. It needed to be brought out. And so I started that. When I started, the idea struck me.

I decided I needed to do something with that store. It was just vacant after being a grocery store. So I was thinking, why didn't I try to do music, have some gatherings. So I made up my mind that is what I'm going to do.

The first two years was in the tiny store that's now the museum. I had bleachers and things just run up the walls. I had an extension built on for concessions. But we eventually tore that down. But I got two hundred people in that little store building.

I just had them hanging from the rafters and every way. The first year, I had it every other Saturday night. One show a night wouldn't take care of it, though. I was trying to have two shows, but they wouldn't go home. They'd just go out and stand on the porch and then come back in with the next bunch. And I finally said, this is ridiculous. I'm gonna have a program every Saturday night. And I'm going to quit my job as a cook at the school. It was kind of scary to quit the work you had. My children looked at me like I was losing my mind.

So I talked to my brother, Joe, my mother, and I told them what I wanted to do is have a music hall built. So Joe designed the building. We had quite a bit of hired help. We had volunteer help. We had our Mother's help. And a little bit later on down the line, we had June and John's help with the finances. My idea was to preserve the acoustic music. It would have been wrong to have any other kind of music besides what my Mother and Daddy and Maybelle done.

And then I called the paper and talked to the Bristol paper and the Kingsport paper and the Johnson City paper. And I said, "I'll tell you what I'm fixing to do." And I said, "I'd be glad for you to run an article." They said, "Well, Miss Carter, we sure will." So all three papers come out with what I was trying to do.

Well, I looked down the road. I was setting down there on the step. And I thought, "Lord God, there may not be nobody come." And then I saw the cars coming up the road and they overflowed. The building overflowed.

And I remembered what my Daddy told me. He wished I'd try to carry on the music. And I thought, well, I told Daddy what I'd do. And I said, "Now God, me and you'll have a talk. I want to tell you what I'm a gonna do." And I said, "I'll never do nothing that'd bring dishonor to my people or to you. So I made two vows and I've kept them both.

So that was my goal. I just kept on. It was very little

money I had to work with. Admission the first year was a dollar. And then children, they've always more or less come in free up until about twelve, and then we increased it to five dollars for adults, and a child six to twelve a dollar.

But from the start, I just had control. I don't think thirty years I've ever had to call the law over ten times. I just make it plain that's the way it's going to be. And if anybody ever comes in under the influence of alcohol and gets up on the stage and tells a dirty joke, I stop it. Stop my music. Or to start dancing that ain't very becoming. I stop that. I think everybody down here's kinda afraid of me.

I don't know how it went on and on and on. It would be awful hard to close because they come from all over the world. And I thought I ought to quit. I'm tired. But I don't know exactly how to.

My oldest son said, "Well, Mother, you could quit. You'd have to sit there at that window looking out at that building from now on. And you'd be sitting there tacking a quilt. I know you." I guess I won't quit. I guess I'll just keep trying.

I'm just walking in the shadow of what they done.

JOE CARTER: This is the Fold building. That is where we are at — I gave it the name the Carter Family Fold. A lot of people have asked me what the Fold signifies. And I told them, just like in the Bible, the sheep's fold, it's a place of refuge that offers shelter.

It took a lot of work, sweat, you know. I was working at construction work anyway, building schools and churches. I knew quite a bit about the work and all pertaining. The money was the biggest thing. So that's the reason it's got to be rustic and cheap. I had to take the cheaper ground. I had my work cut out for me.

But you know, it started out over in that little building. And the floor is just shaking when they was dancing. It's a wonder it hadn't broke through, you know, from overloading the thing.

BILL CLIFTON — Musician/Carter Family Friend:
I was so happy when they built the Fold, because I knew it was exactly what A.P. wanted. He always wanted music to be available here in the valley. And music comes first. And he wanted live music. Janette could have done it the way he did it, which is just to have a summer park and just do it in the summertime. But no, she chose to do it on a year 'round basis.

So it was built with love, completely.

And that's the other thing A.P. would have always wanted. It wasn't a commercial thing. It was built with love.

DALE JETT — A.P. and Sara Carter's Grandson:
Absolutely a lot of people come to the Fold. I make jokes that some people travel thousands of miles to see a program. Some people come to hear the music. And some people come to look at the dancers. Some people come to people-watch, to just look at the different walks of life. What's the common thread that brings so many different types of people together under one roof? The common thread is music.

But for the local people it's a place they come to have a hotdog. That's their supper. They visit with the neighbors. And it really doesn't matter who's playing. They never look at the marquee. They never look at the papers. It's just we're going to the Fold to visit with friends and have some dinner. And you know it's more of a gathering place.

It's a place where people feel really comfortable whether it be your first time or your hundredth time. A lot of people mention to me how comfortable they feel there. So I think it's really important. I'm not sure what the actual definition of Fold was. I know Joe referred to the sheep returning to the fold. What he had in mind was a place for friends and family to return to. And it seems to have been that because people continue to return.

RITA FORRESTER: We're gonna do whatever we can do. We've been left a tremendous legacy and it's overwhelming sometimes. It's even somewhat frightening because you could never live up to the standards that they set down. You know, it's intimidating, a little bit frightening. And I never saw myself helping with the Carter Fold. I never thought about being so active and doing that. But I love my Mom. And I worshipped my granddad. And she made him the promise that she would carry on his music, which she's done through the Fold. And if I don't try to do everything that I can, them I'm letting both of them down in a very big way.

But to do anything but try our very hardest, we'd be doing all of them a disservice. So we've got to do what we have to do to keep it going. Well, I think that means certainly keeping the Carter Fold, having a weekly performance every week of all time acoustic mountain music that's just the way they played it, making sure that their music is a big part of it.

You know keeping this cabin open so that people can see the real humble beginnings of country music, because this speaks to where country music got its start.

You look at country music today, and it's nothing like it was then. But if there's a symbol at the beginnings of country music, we're sitting in it today. And so, it's important that we keep that open, keep the museum open, and just basically have a place where all these people come to that really have come all my life.

You can come and see the gravestones, and that's fine. They're here. But it's not something that's living and breathing. But when you come to the Carter Fold, you see their music. And it's alive. And I think that's the greatest tribute. I can't think of a better one.

In the store building where we started the music, or when Mom started in the early 1970's, I think it felt like being in the Carter Family's living room.

But I think they still feel like you're listening, like you're visiting in someone's home. It's very down home. It's not commercialized. It's from the heart. It's very real. It's not amplified. It's not electric. Of course, John did some electric concerts. But in the last part of his life all his concerts were acoustic. It was just him and his guitar, and that's what people see. They see the very basics of music, where it started, how beautiful it is with nothing to enhance it or make it anything more than just what it is: someone singing from the heart.

Joe Carter died on March 2, 2005. The following year, on January 22nd, Janette Carter passed away. The Carter Family Fold is their lasting legacy.

DALE JETT: Mother passed on a Sunday. It's almost like she willed herself to live through one more Saturday night — "I'm not leaving on a Saturday night." The funeral arrangements went until Thursday of that week. And then the Saturday performance came around. It was kind of unspoken — "Let's get through each day at a time." But we all knew that the show had to go on. Joe would have wanted it. Mother would have wanted it. They wouldn't have forgiven us had we not had a normal show. Matter of fact, I don't think it was ever spoken. I think everyone assumed that this was the way it was gonna be, and no one questioned it. And we just had the show. And it was difficult, no question about it. But afterwards, it felt like the right thing to do. And I certainly hope that it pleased mother and Joe, and I feel like it did.

The Carter Family

Chapter Twelve — The Legacy

The deaths of Maybelle in 1978 and Sara in 1979 marked the end of an era but not the end of interest in their music. In many ways, the Carter music is more popular than ever.

RITA FORRESTER — A.P. and Sara Carter's Granddaughter: It's the basis for so much music. That's what people don't understand. The Carter Family is like the groundwork. You can't talk to any musician who has not been influenced by the Carter Family. Even Mick Jagger at his mother's funeral sang "Will the Circle Be Unbroken." And I asked him why he sang that. And he said, "I don't know. It just felt like the right thing to do."

Bob Dylan will tell you he was very influenced by the Carter Family. The first thing he asked Johnny Cash when he met him was, "Did you ever meet A.P. Carter?" And of course John said, "I hated to tell him that, no, I hadn't. I didn't get to."

But he has now I think. I think he has now.

CARLENE CARTER — June Carter's Daughter: The thing about the Carter Family that was important to me as an artist is that they really encouraged me as a child to be unique and to make my own Carter Family music. And my momma always said, "Everything that you do is Carter Family music." So we've done some interesting Carter Family music, in that sense. And I felt that responsibility over the years and always tried to honor that and still try to.

And I know grandma was really proud of me when I got my first record deal. It was just always be yourself. Always be true to yourself. And be unique. You don't have to be just like us. But, you have to carry it on. And that's important. And don't let people forget about all this music.

JOHN CARTER CASH — June Carter & Johnny Cash's Son: My parents took me on stage the first time when I was an infant. They brought me out the moment I could walk and told me to take a bow. And it was in my blood to be on stage and perform for people. In some ways, it's a long-standing family tradition. And these songs that I sing are a family tradition. I honestly love and appreciate the Carter music. I honestly love and appreciate many, many kinds of music. I'm not afraid to go anywhere and do anything that my heart so desires. And that can be a very broad range for me. And that comes from my family. That's the way they were.

CARLENE CARTER: My little granddaughter, Annie, Anita Grace, had just had her first guitar recital. And she played "Will the Circle Be Unbroken" at her guitar recital. And so, I feel like it's time for me to start telling her where that comes from, and my other granddaughter, Luna. They both are interested in music. It's their turn to start learning about this, the same age I was when I was learning about this stuff. It needs to be passed down.

I was just losing it at her recital. And I thought, Oh, Grandma June would be loving that. And Grandma Carter would be loving that. And Grandma's loving it.

DALE JETT — A.P. and Sara Carter's Grandson:
I grew up as a Carter. And I grew up in and around music all my life. There was a guitar or harp or fiddle or banjo leaning in every corner. I mean, there was always musical instruments around any home that belonged to the Carters. If you wanted to play music, there it was. And you were more than welcome. So I took it for granted a lot.

I find myself knowing melodies to a lot of the Carter family songs though I never started playing music myself till I was in my twenties. But I just took it for granted and never really paid attention to it till Mother started having shows at the Fold. Then, of course, I got involved and started meeting the musicians and made a lot of great friends and started to really understand how much I appreciated the music. And I didn't realize how much I knew melodies to a lot of the songs having heard them in growing up. Now I look back at myself. And at twenty years old, I suddenly found this interest. So I'm hopeful that my son will pick up the interest.

But even if not, I would hope that there are people who will. Their last name doesn't have to be Carter to carry that torch. To keep that music alive is certainly my hope. I don't care what their last names are.

RANDY SCRUGGS - Musician, Carter & Cash Family Friend:
I think the important thing to keep in perspective about the Carter Family is that they were real people, they spoke of

real times, and they spoke about it honestly, about how families go through pain and strife and suffering and hard times, yet find the rainbow at the end. There was hope there. Musically I think what they did represents the true roots of country music in the tone of certain instruments. You know, if I musically get lost somewhere or get off on some tangent, just when it feels like I'm not focused I can sit down and play an early Carter Family song, and it just seems to center me. It brings me back to a certain point, a grounding point. So I know how important that's been for me, and for other people, both people in the music industry, but also people who couldn't whistle Dixie.

PEGGY BULGER — Folklorist:
If you say: Why are the Carters so important? I would say, "Well, why is Bach important? Why is Sousa important?" The Carters are just as important. They're iconic. They are in our musical repertoire, so ingrained that it plays in our minds all the time but we're not even really conscious of it. We go, "I know that." Chances are people know a great deal of the Carter repertoire but they've never put it together that it comes from them. It's part of our musical legacy.

By knowing the story of the Carters I think you're just learning to be culturally literate in the United States. You can't really look at American music without knowing about the Carters or certain people that have just made such a big impact. It's just like Elvis. Why study Elvis? Let's face it. The world was never the same after him, never the same after the Carters, the Beatles. There are certain groups that have had such a big impact on music and made a big turning point in music.

ROSANNE CASH — Musician and Carter Family In-Law:
I'm not blood-related to the Carters. My dad is Johnny Cash and he married a Carter, June Carter. And by way of his respect and his marriage I came to understand who the Carter Family was, and their importance, and I developed a profound love and respect for this body of music, which I think is so American. It's one of the things we have as Americans that is truly ours, that we drew from Celtic roots and Elizabethan poetry and those things we brought over and distilled that are so us, that's so part of who we are as Americans. And this lexicon is so powerful, it's the bedrock that gave birth to country music, and the wider realm of folk music, and without the Carter Family, I hesitate to say there wouldn't be any roots music, but it certainly wouldn't be what it is.

JOHNNY CASH — Carter Family In-Law:
People say they don't know the Carters and yet they're singing their songs. Saying "Who are they?" and they're singing their songs. I've seen that so many times. We'd hear a song, June and I would, and then June would start singing a Carter family song that was the same tune as a new song that just came out. It blew me away every time she'd do that. We'd turn on the radio, and there wouldn't be three songs passed, and June would start singing a Carter family song to the tune of the one that was playing. It was a mean thing to do [chuckles], but it was very rewarding, very revealing.

MIKE SEEGER — Musician and Carter Family Friend:
I think there's a lot of layers to the value of the Carter Family. They were possibly the first group to sell a large number

of records of mountain singing. They sold hundreds of thousands of records back in the late Twenties until the Depression.

And what was it in their music? Well, I think the most important thing is that there's something we can't talk about — sound charisma — that some people just have that communicates. Whether it's Bob Dylan, Johnny Cash, or my brother Pete or the Beatles, or whomever, there's just a certain something that you can talk about for ages and ages and ages.

Three exceptional people getting together to make something that's even more exceptional. A group which sings unlike any other group on record that has a certain way of singing and a certain rhythmic guitar backup. Sara was a remarkable singer and Maybelle, her pal from childhood could sing a very creative harmony, something that would not intrude at all but would just add to it. And A.P. bringing up the bottom just every now and then. It gives you the feeling of a family, it gives the feeling of country, but it gives you something that's timeless.

I mean, what more testimony do you need than having everything they ever recorded plus some radio transcriptions still in print some seventy-five years later? It's amazing.

You don't have many people who have made recordings from that era or from any era who live on that way.

But one of the biggest things about the Carter Family is the feeling of mystery. How did they do that? How did they create that wonderful music?

CHARLES WOLFE — Music Historian:

You can look at them historically as great artists because they were great synthesizers, like all great American musicians were. They took church music that they had learned as kids, they took the old ballads that they heard in Leicester County, they heard the blues that their friend Lesley Riddle would sing, they would take the old pop songs that they would find people singing back in the hills, and they would take all this together, mix it up, and they would make their own special arrangements, create harmonies, and create a sound that is in many ways the archetypal country music sound. So as a result, from an historical point of view, they are important. But from a more visceral point of view, the Carter Family created songs that were so appealing, and so enduring, that they almost immediately went back in to the folk tradition from whence they sprung. And so today whether it's a small country show out in a barn someplace or a TV show or a bluegrass festival, people everywhere still sing Carter Family songs. The number of artists who have done Carter Family albums is too numerous to count. Their songs are eminently singable, and they are very comfortable, they are like your favorite pair of shoes that's nice and broken in. And a Carter Family song is something that makes you feel warm and comfortable and kind of reminds you of all the good things that this culture brought to us.

Many of these songs that the Carters did have became so popular that a lot of people almost think of them as folk songs — "Storms are on the Ocean," "Will the Circle Be Unbroken," "On the Rock where Moses Stood," "Engine 143," "John Hardy was a Desperate Little Man." You can go through Harry Smith's Anthology of American Folk Music and just tick off the Carter songs. And when you look at people who came along as the second generation of country musicians —— people like the Stanley Brothers, and Bill Monroe, and Flatt and Scruggs — they all held the Carter Family up as gods. I remember when Flatt and Scruggs invited Mother Maybelle to be a guest on their TV show. Earl Scruggs was standing there in just rapt admiration watching Mother Maybelle play her big ol' Gibson guitar. And it was really wonderful to see.

So, what has happened is that their songs have broken loose from their original moorings. So people remember "Will the Circle Be Unbroken" but they may not know the Carter Family recording of it. People know "Wildwood Flower," but they may not remember the Carter Family recording of it. The songs got loose into the American consciousness. I think even more so than Woody Guthrie songs. They're songs that simply became part of our national repertoire.

I think nothing would have pleased A.P. more. This is exactly what he wanted.

Other Beth Harrington Films

The Winding Stream

Reed

Kam Wah Chung

Searching for York

Beervana

ZigZag

Welcome to the Club – The Women of Rockabilly

The Aleutians: Cradle of the Storms

Digital TV: A Cringley Crash Course

The Blinking Madonna & Other Miracles

The Moveable Feast

Ave Maria

Some Other Books By PFP / AJAR Contemporaries

Blind Tongues - Sterling Watson
the Book of Dreams - Craig Nova
A Russian Requiem - Roland Merullo
Ambassador of the Dead - Askold Melnyczuk
Demons of the Blank Page - Roland Merullo
Celebrities in Disgrace - Elizabeth Searle
(eBook version only)
"Last Call" - Roland Merullo
(eBook "single")
Fighting Gravity - Peggy Rambach
Leaving Losapas - Roland Merullo
Girl to Girl: The Real Deal on Being A Girl Today - Anne Driscoll
Revere Beach Elegy - Roland Merullo
a four-sided bed - Elizabeth Searle
Revere Beach Boulevard - Roland Merullo
Tornado Alley - Craig Nova
"The Young and the Rest of Us" - Elizabeth Searle
(eBook "single")
Lunch with Buddha - Roland Merullo
Temporary Sojourner - Tony Eprile
Passion for Golf:In Pursuit of the Innermost Game - Roland Merullo
What Is Told - Askold Melnyczuk
Talk Show - Jaime Clarke
"What A Father Leaves" - Roland Merullo
(eBook "single" & audio book)
Music In and On the Air - Lloyd Schwartz
The Calling - Sterling Watson
The Family Business - John DiNatale
Taking the Kids to Italy- Roland Merullo
This is Paradise - Suzanne Strempek Shea

6554950R00100

Printed in Great Britain
by Amazon.co.uk, Ltd.,
Marston Gate.